#1

honey

miel

عسل

#2

tuna

thon

ماهی تن

#3

cauliflower

chou-fleur

گل کلم

#4

vegetable

légume

سبزیجات

#5

banana

banane

موز

#6

egg

œuf

تخم‌مرغ

#7

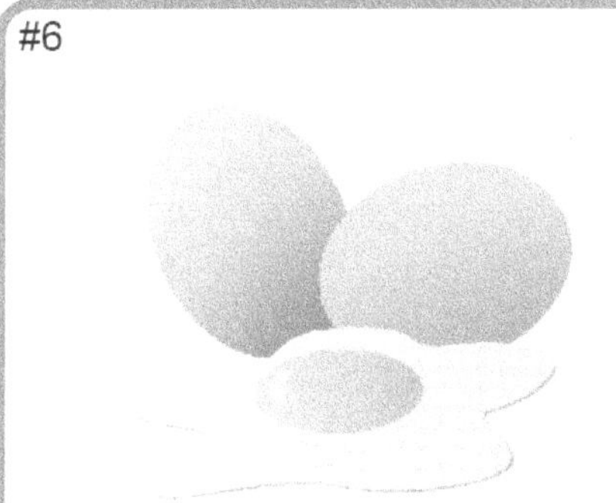

popsicles

esquimaux

بستنی یخی

#8

cake

gâteau

کیک

#9

turnip

navet

شلغم

#10

strawberry

fraise

توت فرنگی

#11

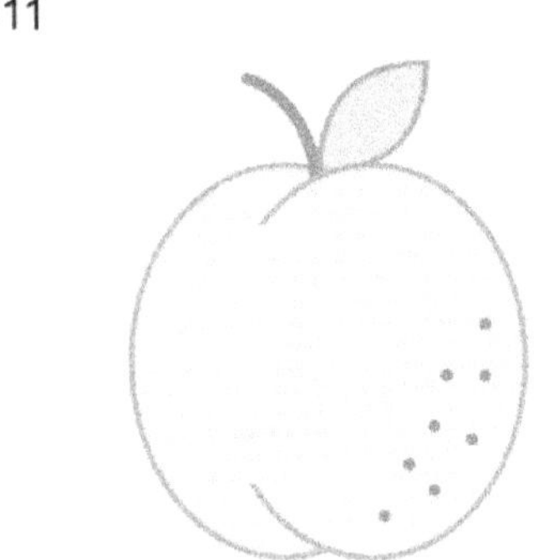

apricot

abricot

زردآلو

#12

yogurt

yaourt

ماست

#13

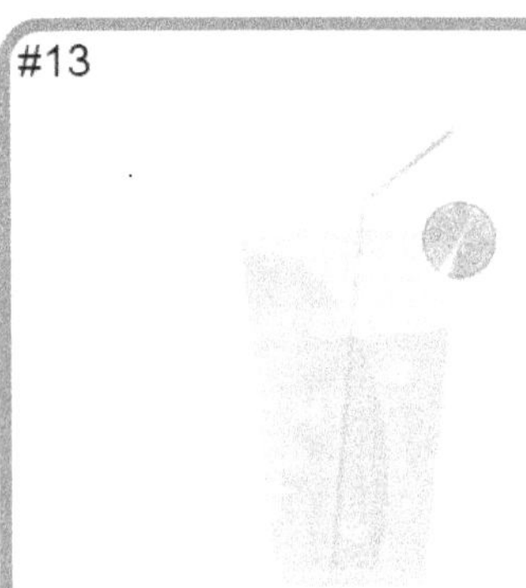

lemonade

limonade

لیموناد

#14

fruit

fruit

میوه

#15

ham

jambon

ژامبون

#16

chocolate

chocolat

شکلات

#17

lime

citron vert

لیموترش

#18

jam

confiture

مربا

#19

water

eau

آب

#20

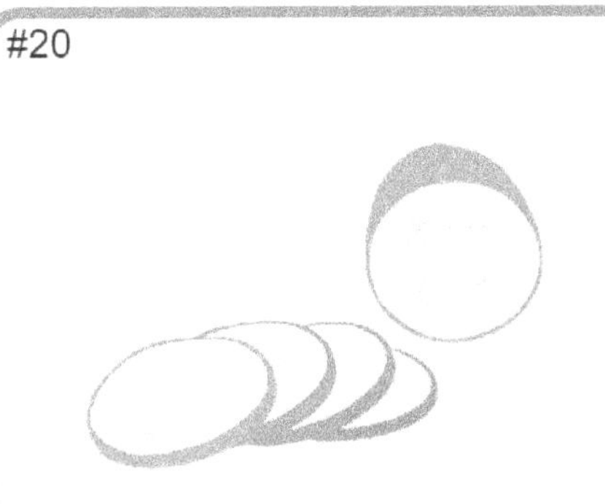

cucumber

concombre

خیار

#21

shrimp

crevette

میگو

#22

salt

sel

نمک

#23

milk

lait

شیر

#24

salad

salade

سالاد

#25

plum

prune

آلو

#26

wheat

blé

گندم

#27

cabbage

chou

کلم

#28

sausage

saucisse

سوسیس

#29

pumpkin

citrouille

کدو تنبل

#30

mushroom

champignon

قارچ

#31

bean

haricot

لوبیا

#32

radish

radis

تربچه

#33

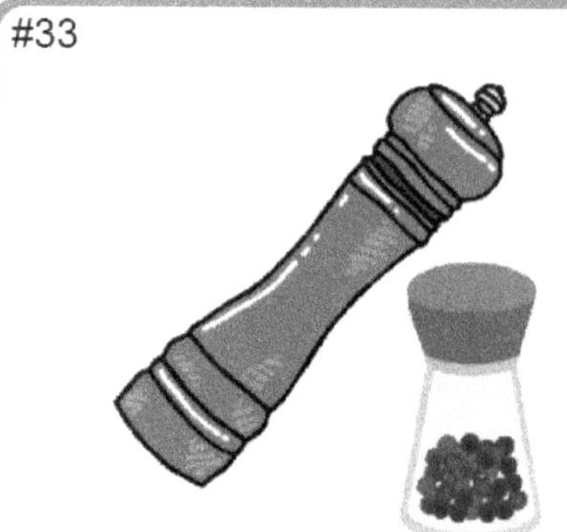

pepper

poivre

فلفل

#34

coconut

noix de coco

نارگیل

#35

sunflower

tournesol

گل آفتابگردان

#36

rice

riz

برنج

#37

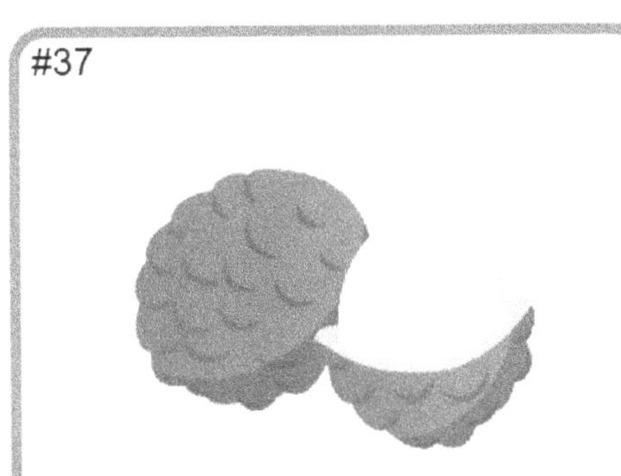

lychee

litchi

لیچی

#38

wine

vin

شراب

#39

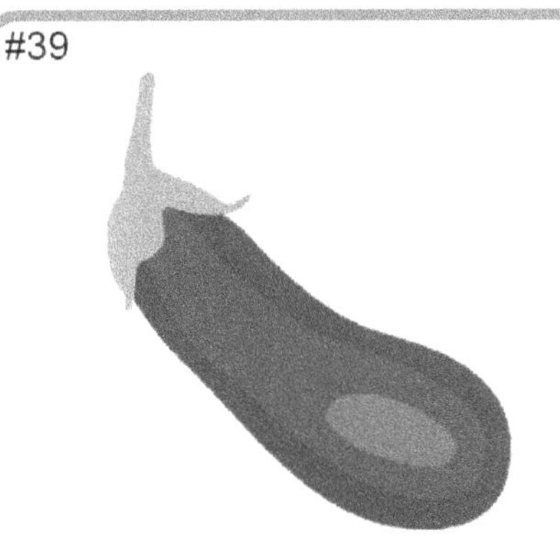

eggplant

aubergine

بادمجان

#40

cookie

biscuit

بیسکویت

#41

pomegranate

grenade

انار

#42

lemon

citron

لیمو

#43

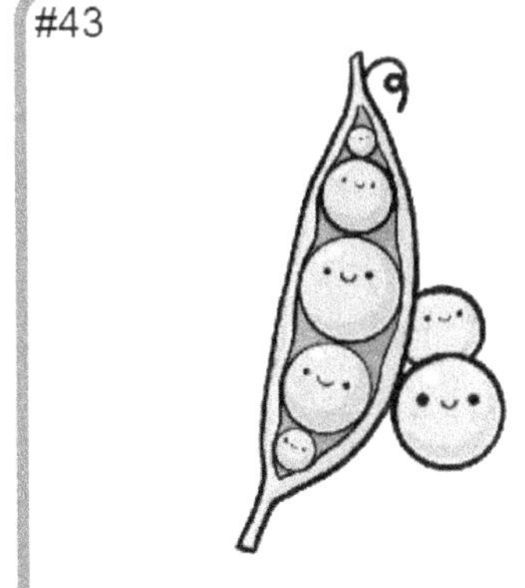

peas

pois

نخود

#44

coffee

café

قهوه

#45

tea

thé

چای

#46

meat

viande

گوشت

#47

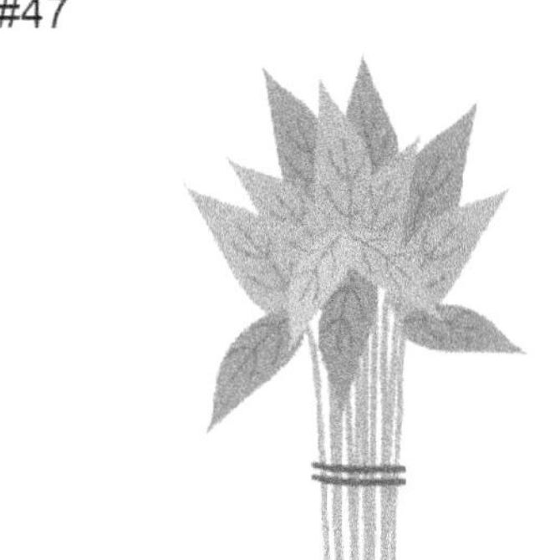

spinach

épinards

اسفناج

#48

grape

raisin

انگور

#49

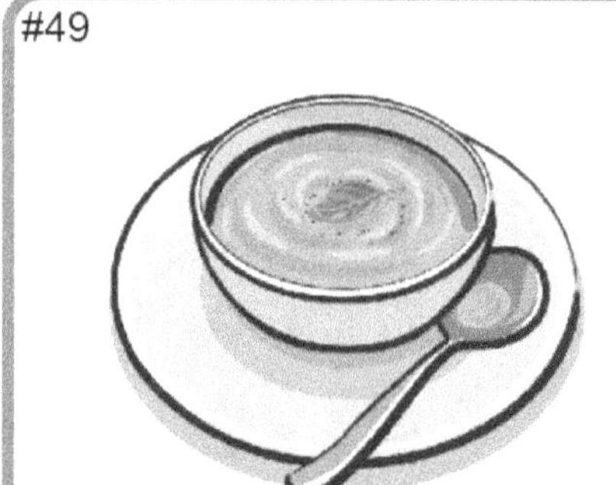

soup

soupe

سوپ

#50

beer

bière

آبجو

#51

watermelon

pastèque

هندوانه

#52

food

nourriture

غذا

#53

bread

pain

نان

#54

broccoli

brocoli

کلم بروکلی

#55

corn

maïs

ذرت

#56

garlic

ail

سیر

#57

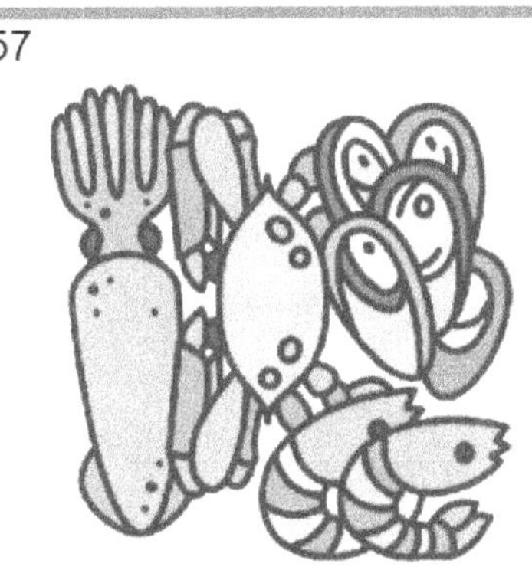

seafood

fruits de mer

غذاهای دریایی

#58

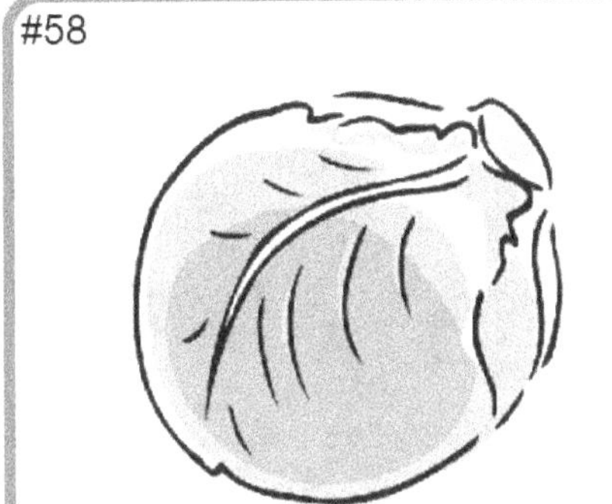

lettuce

laitue

کاهو

#59

potato

pomme de terre

سیب‌زمینی

#60

icecream

crème glacée

بستنی

#61

meal

repas

وعده غذایی

#62

dinner

dîner

شام

#63

celery

céleri

کرفس

#64

tangerine

mandarine

نارنگی

#65

carrot

carotte

هویج

#66

peach

pêche

هلو

#67

peanut

cacahuète

بادام زمینی

#68

noodles

nouilles

نودل

#69

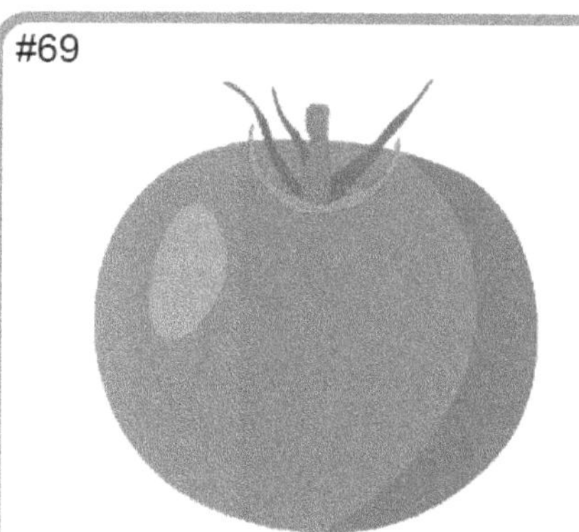

tomato

tomate

گوجه‌فرنگی

#70

onion

oignon

پیاز

#71

raspberry

framboise

تمشک

#72

sugar

sucre

شکر

#73

pear

poire

گلابی

#74

pineapple

ananas

آناناس

#75

candy

bonbon

آب‌نبات

#76

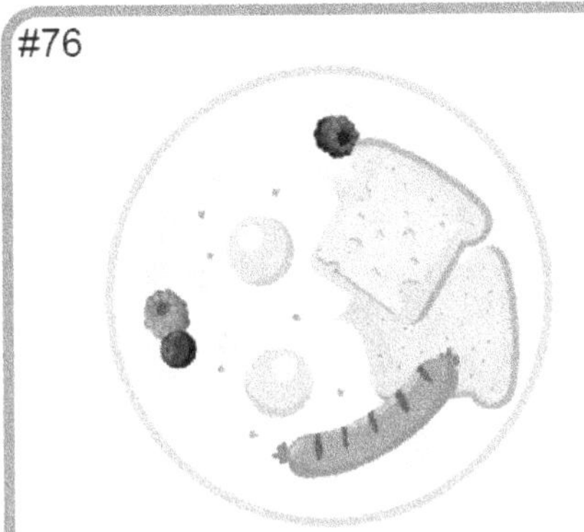

breakfast

petit-déjeuner

صبحانه

#77

apple

pomme

سیب

#78

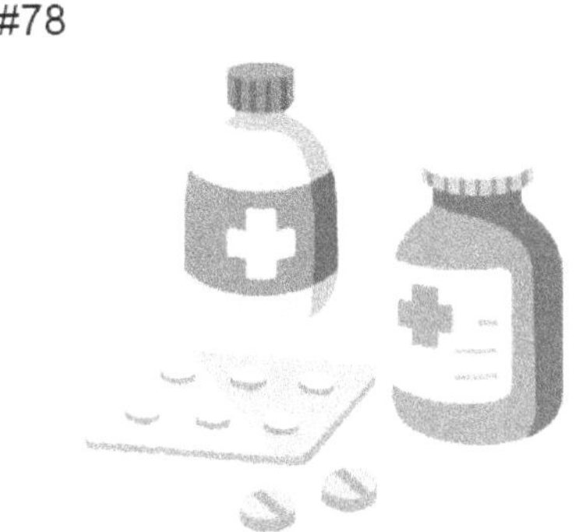

medicine

médicament

دارو

#79

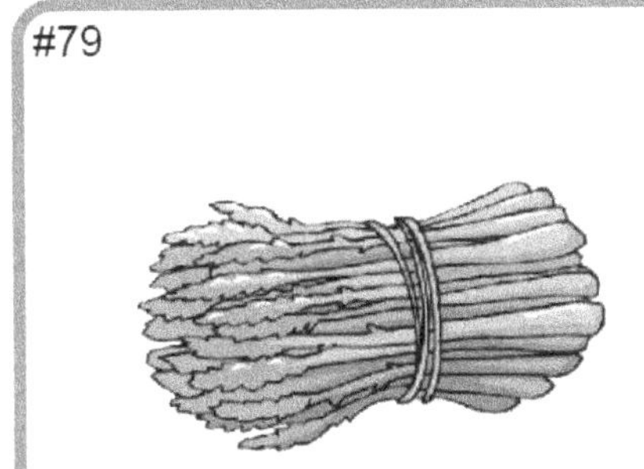

asparagus

asperge

مارچوبه

#80

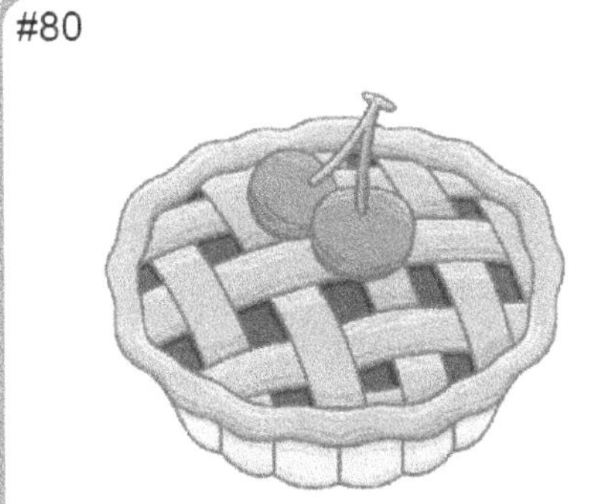

pie

tarte

پای

#81

cheese

fromage

پنیر

#82

juice

jus

آبمیوه

#83

goat

chèvre

بز

#84

tiger

tigre

ببر

#85

dog

chien

سگ

#86

horse

cheval

اسب

#87

monkey

singe

میمون

#88

stork

cigogne

لک‌لک

#89

wasp

guêpe

زنبور سرخ

#90

kitten

chaton

بچه گربه

#91

clam

palourde

صدف

#92

pelican

pélican

پلیکان

#93

fox

renard

روباه

#94

jellyfish

méduse

عروس دریایی

#95

squirrel

écureuil

سنجاب

#96

snail

escargot

حلزون

#97

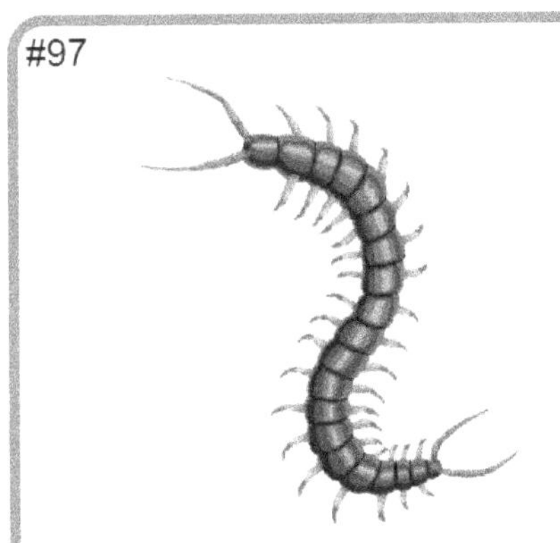

centipede

mille-pattes

هزار پا

#98

dragonfly

libellule

سنجاقک

#99

camel

chameau

شتر

#100

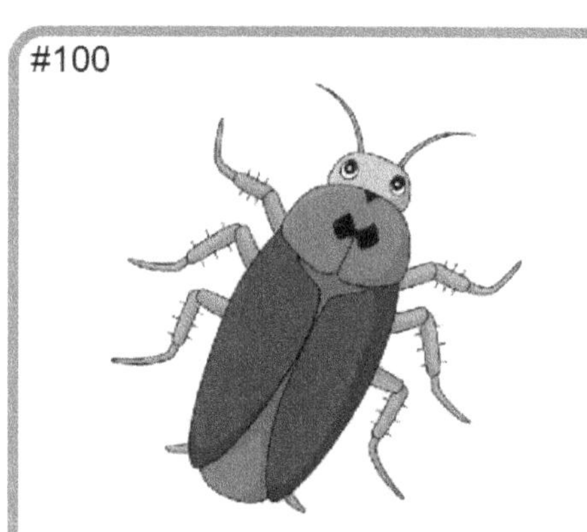

cockroach

cafard

سوسک

#101

ant

fourmi

مورچه

#102

reindeer

renne

گوزن شمالی

#103

cheetah

guépard

یوزپلنگ

#104

sheep

mouton

گوسفند

#105

boar

sanglier

گراز

#106

grasshopper

sauterelle

ملخ

#107

duck

canard

اردک

#108

shark

requin

کوسه

#109

hawk

faucon

شاهین

#110

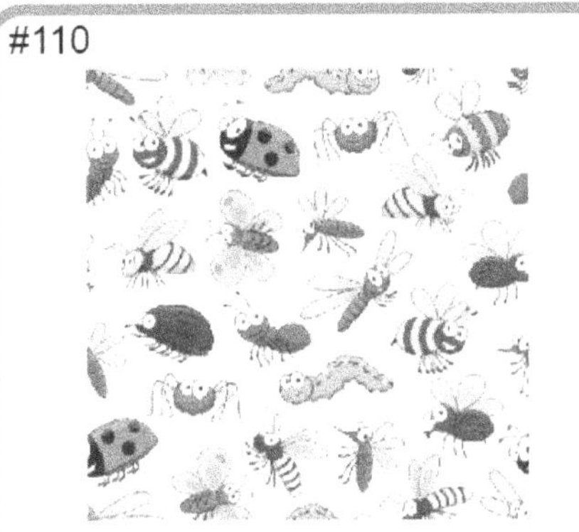

insect

insecte

حشره

#111

lizard

lézard

مارمولک

#112

frog

grenouille

قورباغه

#113

pigeon

pigeon

کبوتر

#114

turkey

dinde

بوقلمون

#115

deer

cerf

گوزن

#116

seagull

mouette

مرغ دریایی

#117

mare

jument

مادیان

#118

octopus

poulpe

اختاپوس

#119

mice

souris

موش‌ها

#120

fish

poisson

ماهی

#121

bee

abeille

زنبور

#122

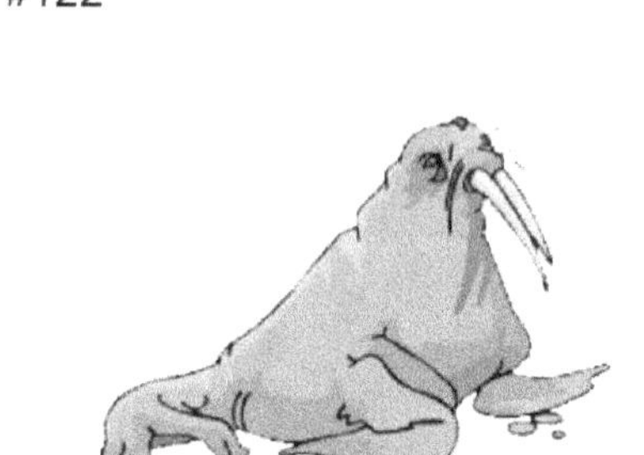

walrus

morse

گراز دریایی

#123

beetle

scarabée

سوسک

#124

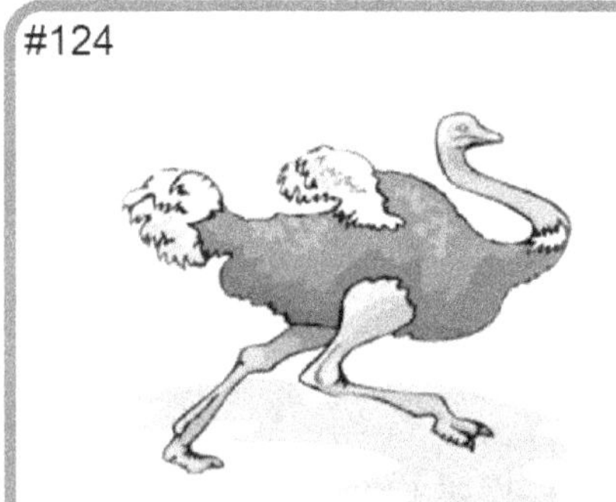

ostrich

autruche

شترمرغ

#125

ladybug

coccinelle

کفش‌دوزک

#126

cat

chat

گربه

#127

crab

crabe

خرچنگ

#128

animal

animal

حیوان

#129

owl

hibou

جغد

#130

squid

calmar

ماهی مرکب

#131

sparrow

moineau

گنجشک

#132

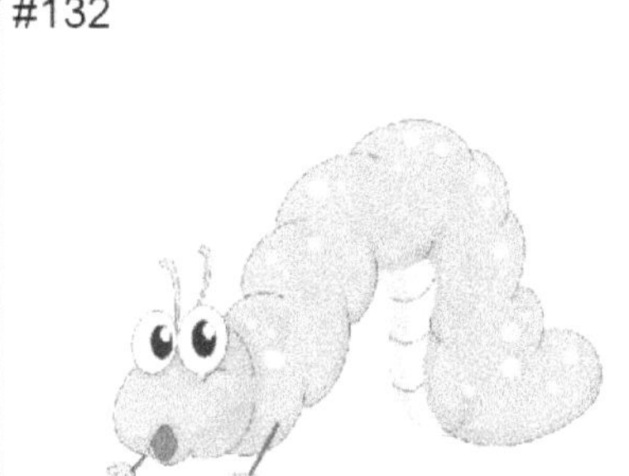

caterpillar

chenille

کرم ابریشم

#133

worm

ver

کرم

#134

eagle

aigle

عقاب

#135

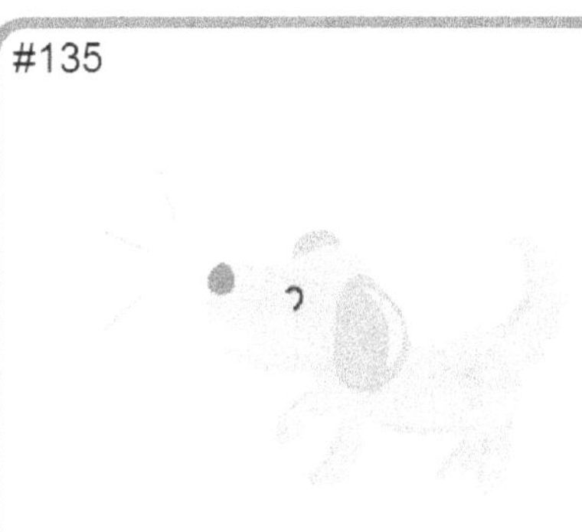

puppy

chiot

توله سگ

#136

swan

cygne

قو

#137

hedgehog

hérisson

جوجه‌تیغی

#138

elephant

éléphant

فیل

#139
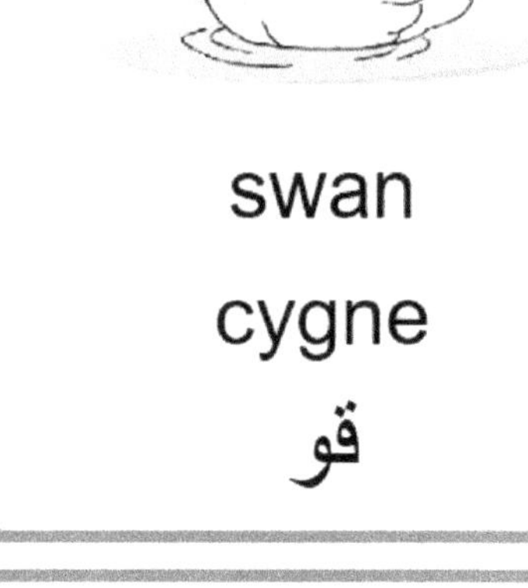

peacock

paon

طاووس

#140

dolphin

dauphin

دلفین

#141

monster

monstre

هیولا

#142

dinosaur

dinosaure

دایناسور

#143

rat

rat

موش

#144

snake

serpent

مار

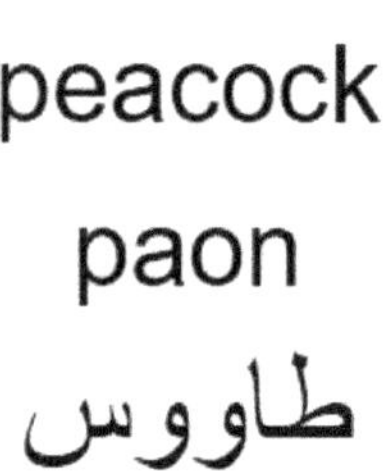

#145

pig

cochon

خوک

#146

lion

lion

شیر

#147

alligator

alligator

تمساح

#148

chicken

poulet

مرغ

#149

unicorn

licorne

تکشاخ

#150

whale

baleine

نهنگ

#151

turtle

tortue

لاکپشت

#152

kangaroo

kangourou

کانگورو

#153

toad

crapaud

وزغ

#154

quail

caille

بلدرچین

#155

lobster

homard

خرچنگ

#156

dove

colombe

قمری

#157

moth

papillon de nuit

شب‌پره

#158

butterfly

papillon

پروانه

#159

vulture

vautour

کرکس

#160

mermaid

sirène

پری دریایی

#161

hen

poule

مرغ

#162

parrot

perroquet

طوطی

#163

mouse

souris

موش

#164

mole

taupe

خال

#165

rooster

coq

خروس

#166

mosquito

moustique

پشه

#167

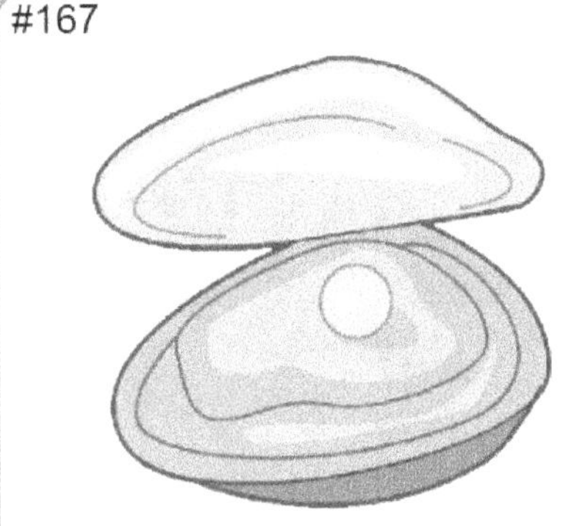

oyster

huître

صدف

#168

hippopotamus

hippopotame

اسب آبی

#169

goose

oie

غاز

#170

cow

vache

گاو

#171

bird

oiseau

پرنده

#172

starfish

étoile de mer

ستاره دریایی

#173

crow

corbeau

کلاغ

#174

spider

araignée

عنکبوت

#175

rabbit

lapin

خرگوش

#176

porcupine

porc-épic

خارپشت

#177

toddler

tout-petit

نوپا

#178

sister

sœur

خواهر

#179

daughter

fille

دختر

#180

brother

frère

برادر

#181

grandson

petit-fils

نوه پسر

#182

stepmother

belle-mère

نامادری

#183

father

père

پدر

#184

group

groupe

گروه

#185

member

membre

عضو

#186

man

homme

مرد

#187

family

famille

خانواده

#188

kid

enfant

بچه

#189

dad

papa

پدر

#190

woman

femme

زن

#191

granddaughter

petite-fille

نوه دختر

#192

stepson

beau-fils

پسر ناتنی

#193

people

personnes

مردم

#194

kids

enfants

بچه‌ها

#195

grandmother

grand-mère

مادربزرگ

#196

child

enfant

کودک

#197

wife

épouse

همسر

#198

nephew

neveu

برادرزاده

#199

cousin

cousin

دخترخاله

#200

niece

nièce

خواهرزاده

#201

lady

dame

بانو

#202

boyfriend

petit ami

دوست پسر

#203

son

fils

پسر

#204

friend

ami

دوست

#205

boy

garçon

پسر

#206

uncle

oncle

دایی

#207

mother

mère

مادر

#208

girl

fille

دختر

#209

aunt

tante

عمه

#210

mom

maman

مادر

#211

children

enfants

بچه‌ها

#212

stepdaughter

belle-fille

دختر ناتنی

#213

girlfriend

petite amie

دوست دختر

#214

raincoat

imperméable

بارانی

#215

suitcase

valise

چمدان

#216

brush

brosse

برس

#217

kitchen

cuisine

آشپزخانه

#218

candle

bougie

شمع

#219

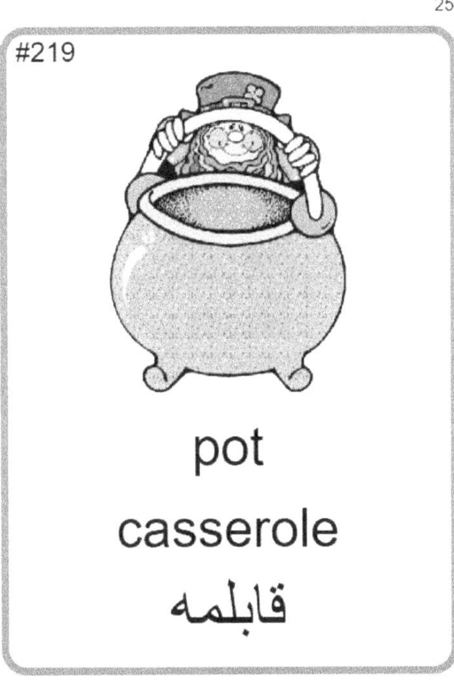

pot

casserole

قابلمه

#220

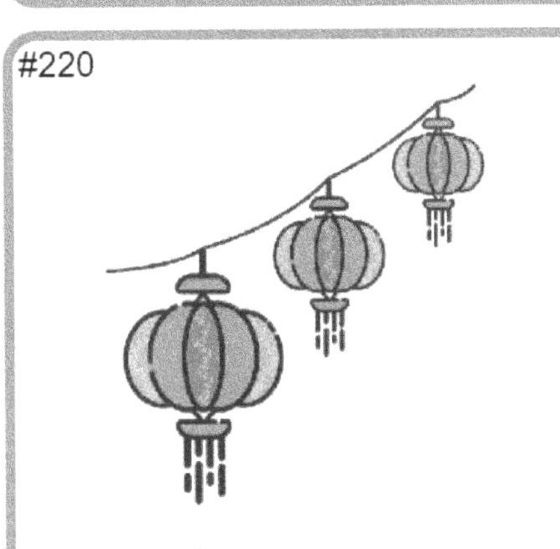

lantern

lanterne

فانوس

#221

letter

lettre

نامه

#222

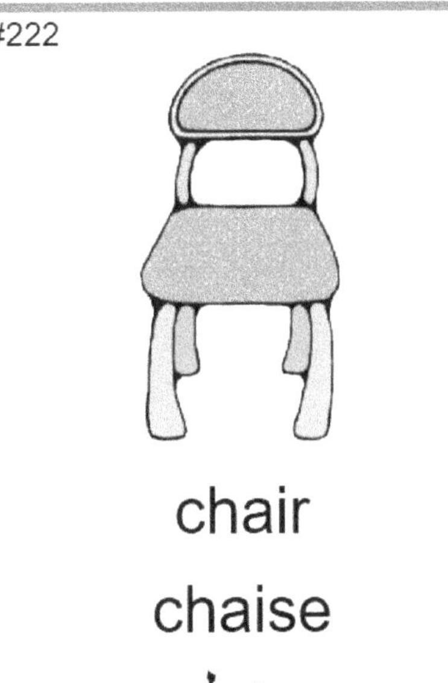

chair

chaise

صندلی

#223

bassinet

berceau

گهواره

#224

broom

balai

جارو

#225

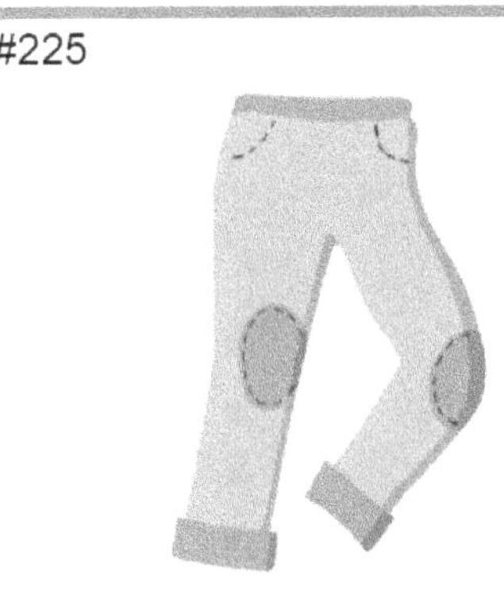

trousers

pantalon

شلوار

#226

closet

placard

کمد لباس

#227

mask

masque

ماسک

#228

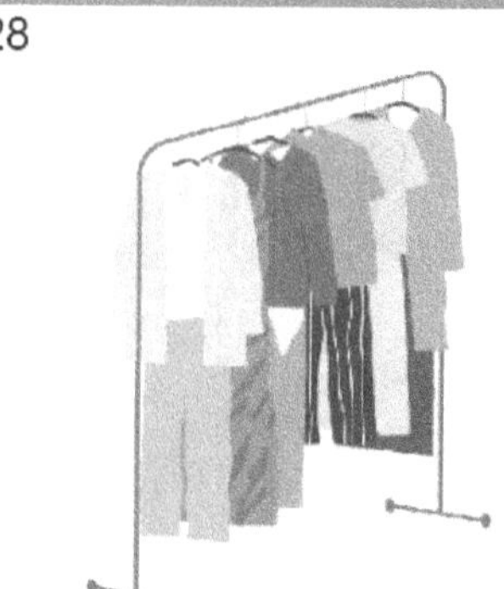

clothes

vêtements

لباس

#229

mirror

miroir

آینه

#230

pajamas

pyjama

لباس خواب

#231

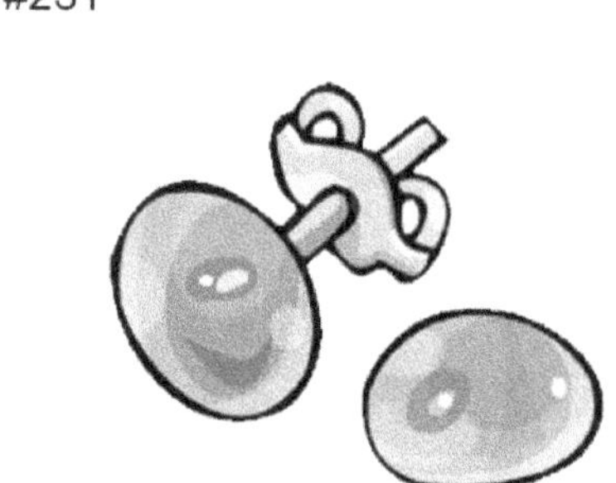

earring

boucle d'oreille

گوشواره

#232

machine

machine

ماشین

#233

briefcase

porte-documents

کیف

#234

collar

collier

یقه

#235

mat

tapis

حصير

#236

toothpaste

dentifrice

خمير دندان

#237

magazine

magazine

مجله

#238

barrel

tonneau

بشكه

#239

pencil

crayon

مداد

#240

compass

boussole

قطب‌نما

#241

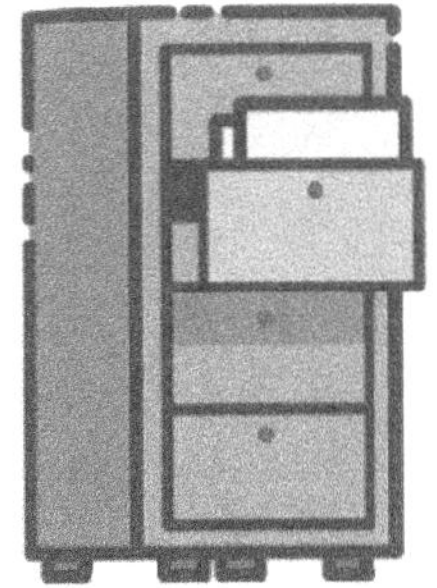

cabinet

armoire

كابينت

#242

cupboard

buffet

قفسه

#243

spoon

cuillère

قاشق

#244

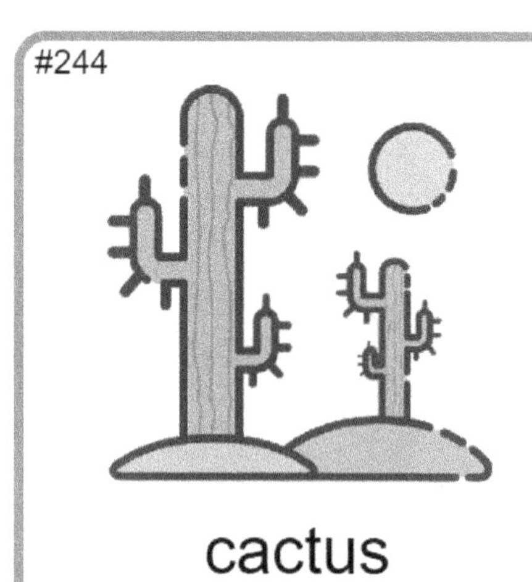

cactus

cactus

كاكتوس

#245

box

boîte

جعبه

#246

chainsaw

tronçonneuse

ارهبرقى

#247

photo

photo

عكس

#248

book

livre

كتاب

#249

dish

plat

ظرف

#250

dice

dés

تاس

#251

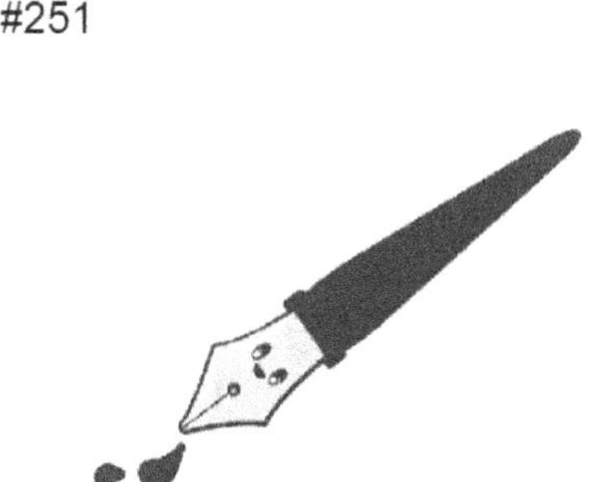

pen

stylo

خودكار

#252

alcohol

alcool

الكل

#253

bookshelf

étagère

قفسه کتاب

#254

strainer

passoire

صافی

#255

rug

tapis

فرش

#256

coat

manteau

کت

#257

plate

assiette

بشقاب

#258

stove

cuisinière

اجاق

#259

picture

image

تصویر

#260

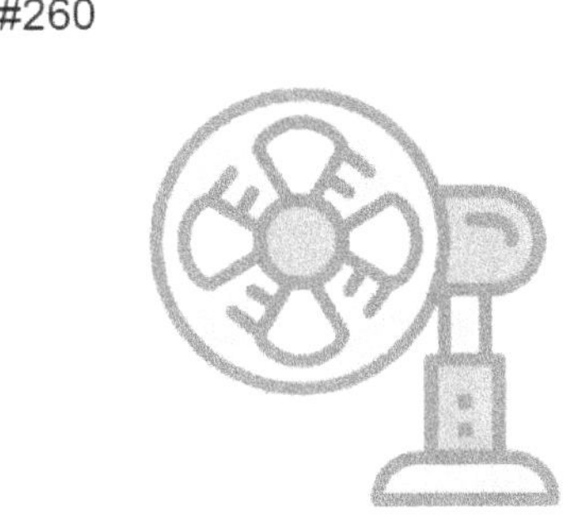

fan

ventilateur

پنکه

#261

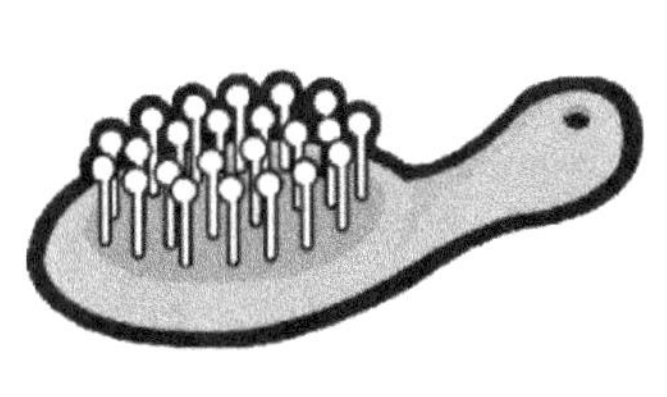

comb

peigne

شانه

#262

boot

botte

چکمه

#263

shirt

chemise

پیراهن

#264

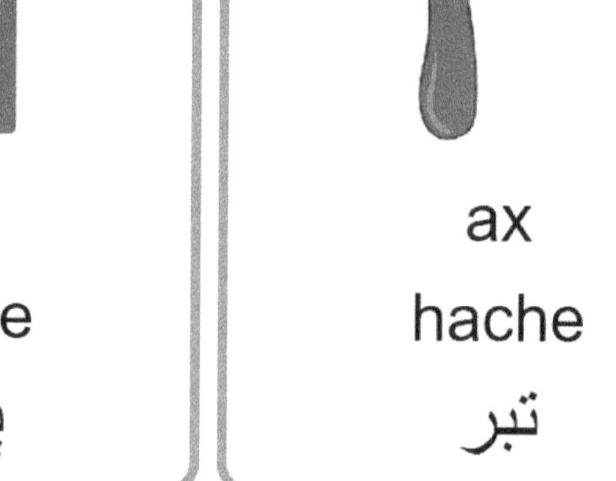

ax

hache

تبر

#265

device

appareil

دستگاه

#266

microphone

microphone

میکروفون

#267

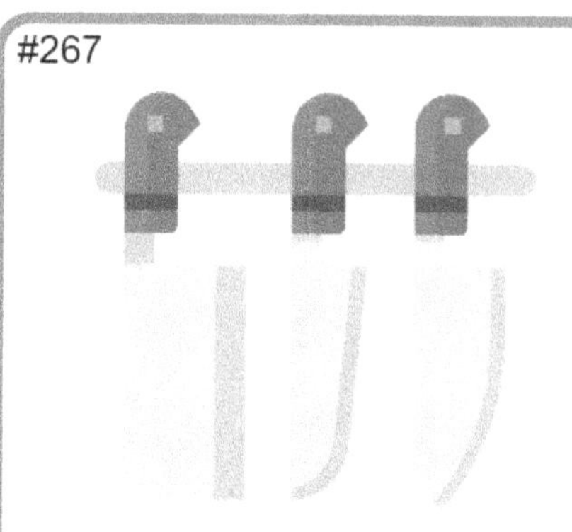

knife

couteau

چاقو

#268

oven

four

فر

#269

cup

tasse

فنجان

#270

lightbulb

ampoule

لامپ

#271

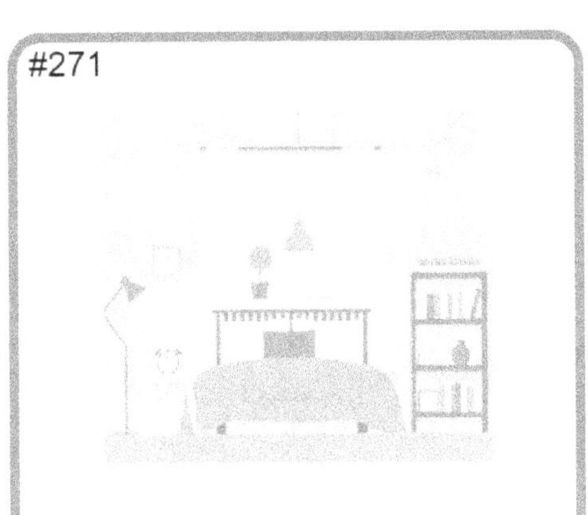

bedroom

chambre

اتاق خواب

#272

newspaper

journal

روزنامه

#273

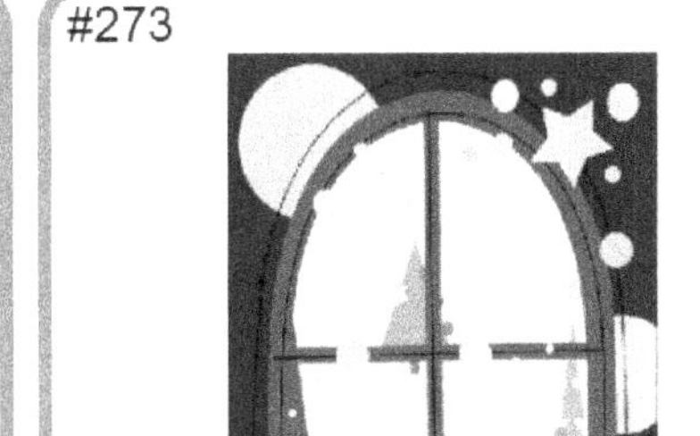

window

fenêtre

پنجره

#274

phone

téléphone

تلفن

#275

silk

soie

ابریشم

#276

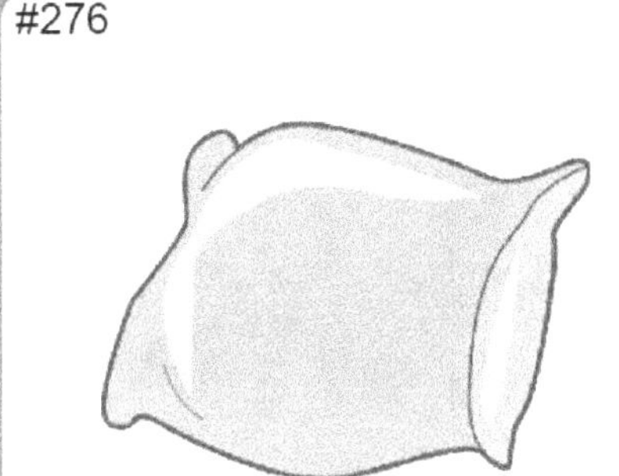

pillow

oreiller

بالش

#277

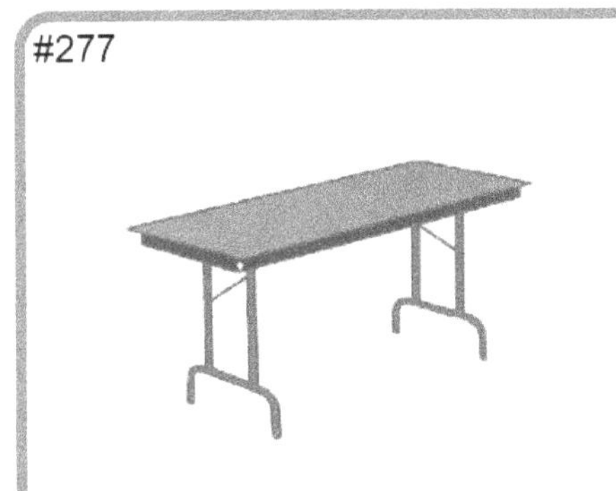

table

table

میز

#278

towel

serviette

حوله

#279

socks

chaussettes

جوراب

#280

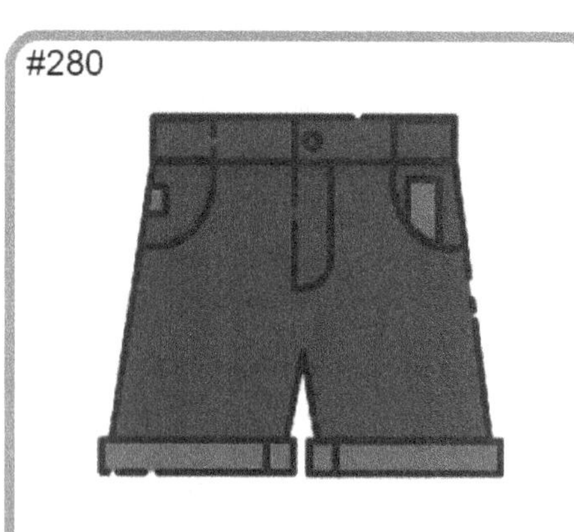

shorts

short

شلوارک

#281

shoes

chaussures

کفش

#282

underpants

slip

زیرشلواری

#283

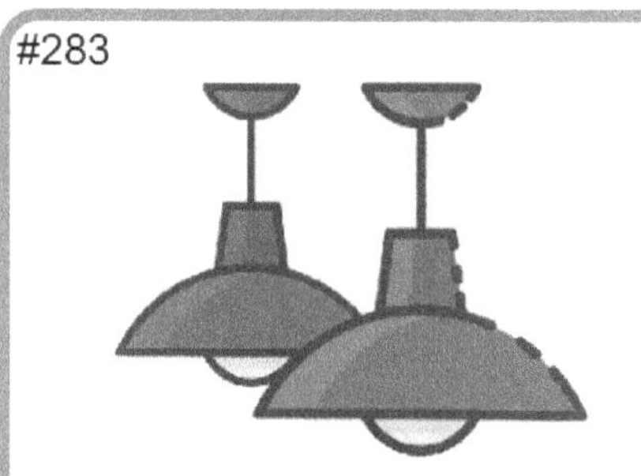

lamp

lampe

لامپ

#284

mug

tasse

ماگ

#285

fireplace

cheminée

شومینه

#286

gasoline

essence

بنزین

#287

teacup

tasse à thé

فنجان چای

#288

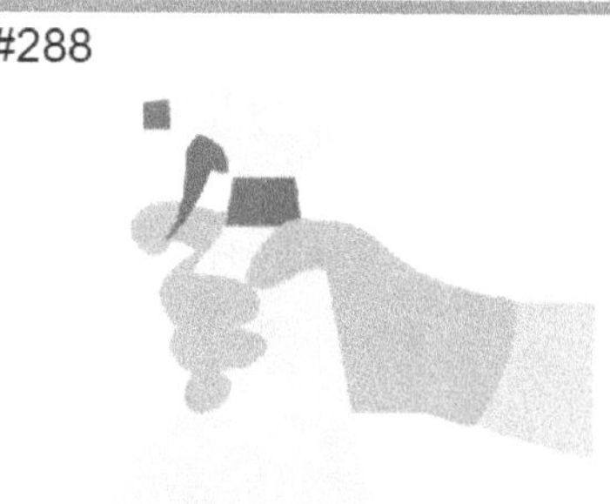

cleanser

nettoyant

پاک‌کننده

#289

bathtub

baignoire

وان حمام

#290

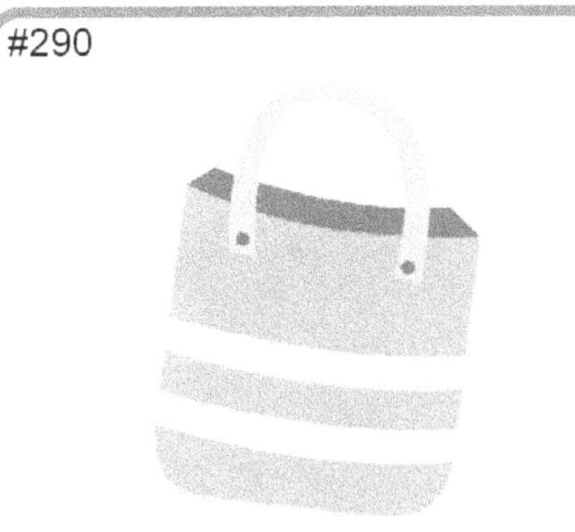

bag

sac

کیف

#291

diaper

couche

پوشک

#292

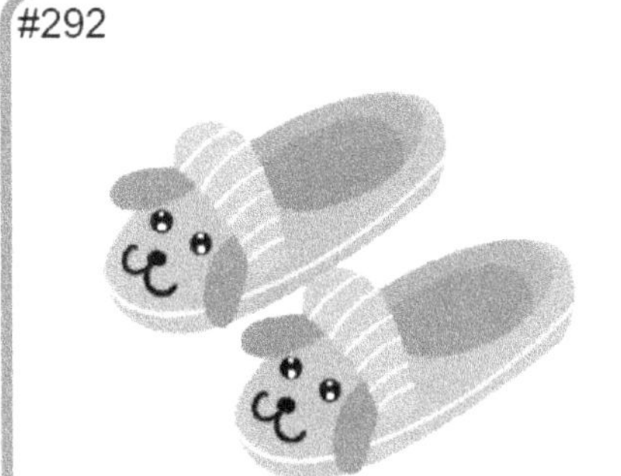

slippers

chaussons

دمپایی

#293

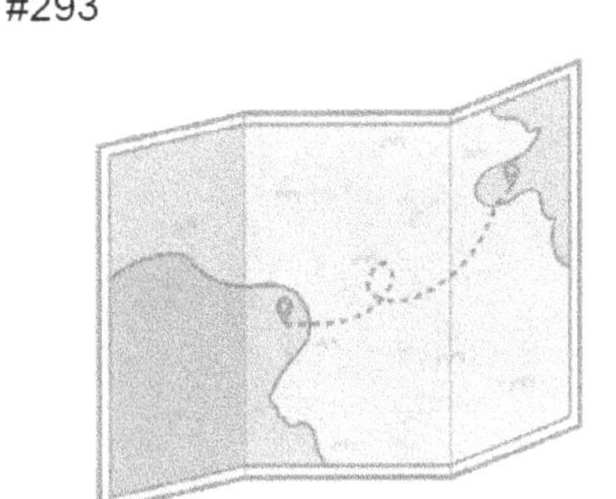

map

carte

نقشه

#294

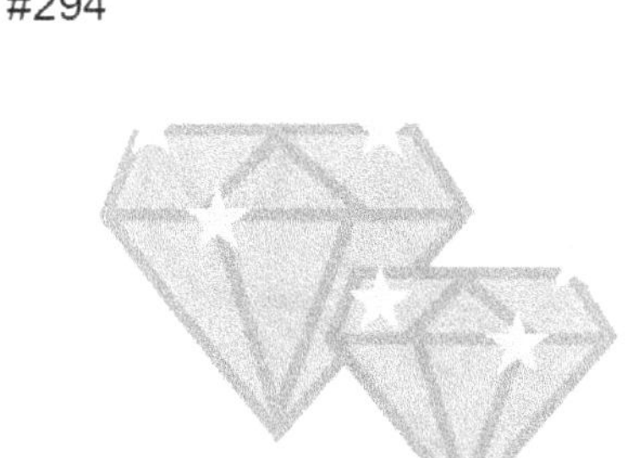

diamond

diamant

الماس

#295

vaccine

vaccin

واکسن

#296

cushion

coussin

کوسن

#297

telephone

téléphone

تلفن

#298

bomb

bombe

بمب

#299

pin

épingle

سنجاق

#300

hat

chapeau

کلاه

#301

wrench

clé

آچار

#302

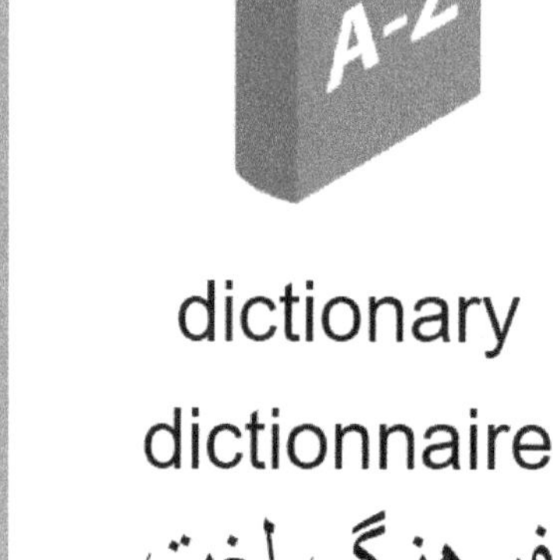

dictionary

dictionnaire

فرهنگ لغت

#303

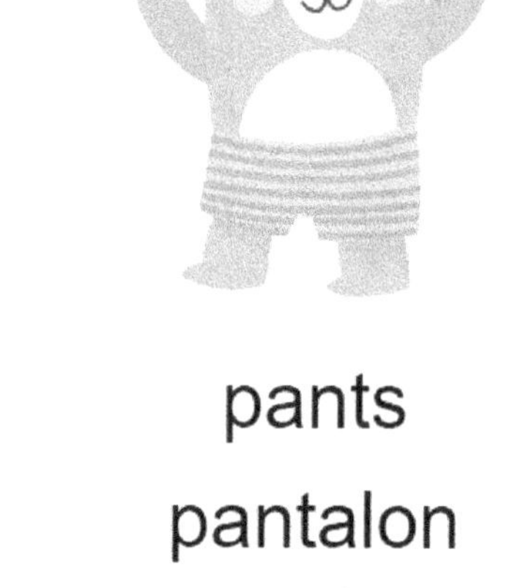

pants

pantalon

شلوار

#304

soap

savon

صابون

#305

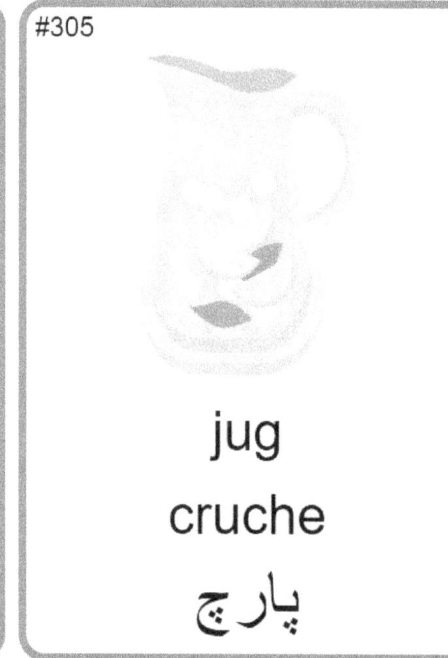

jug

cruche

پارچ

#306

teapot

théière

قوری

#307

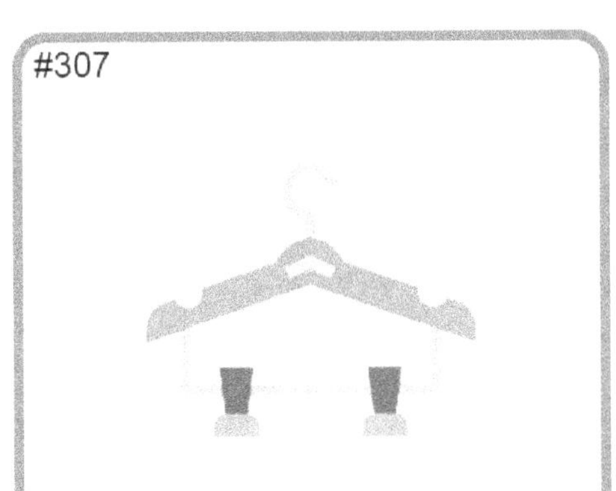

hanger

cintre

چوب رختی

#308

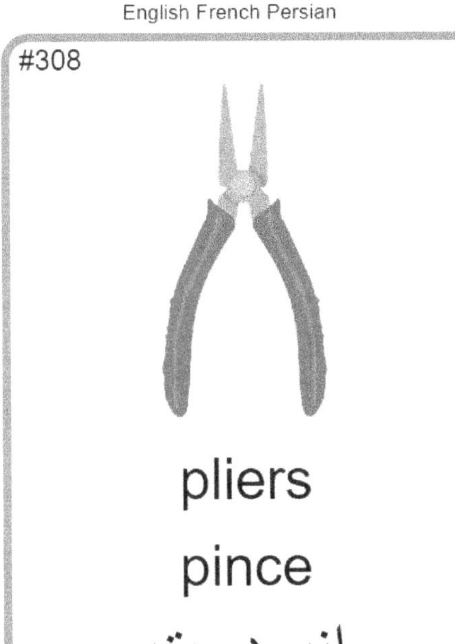

pliers

pince

انبردست

#309

blanket

couverture

پتو

#310

toy

jouet

اسباب بازی

#311

telescope

télescope

تلسکوپ

#312

typewriter

machine à écrire

ماشین تحریر

#313

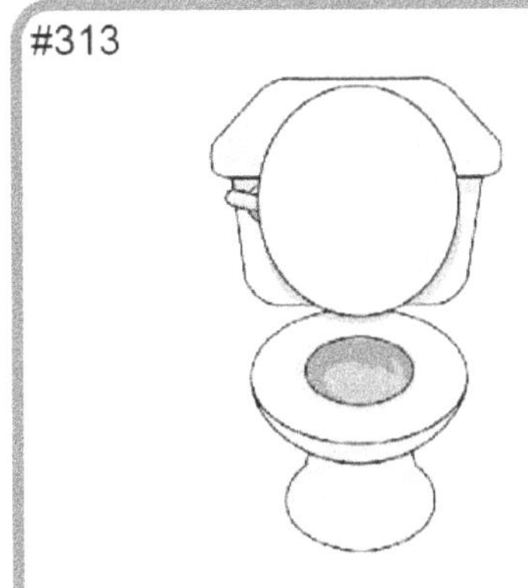

toilet

toilettes

دستشویی

#314

yarn

fil

نخ

#315

dress

robe

لباس

#316

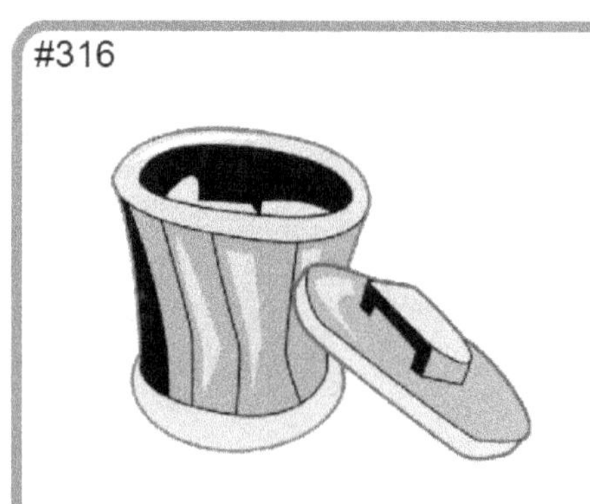

lid

couvercle

درپوش

#317

sweater

pull

ژاکت

#318

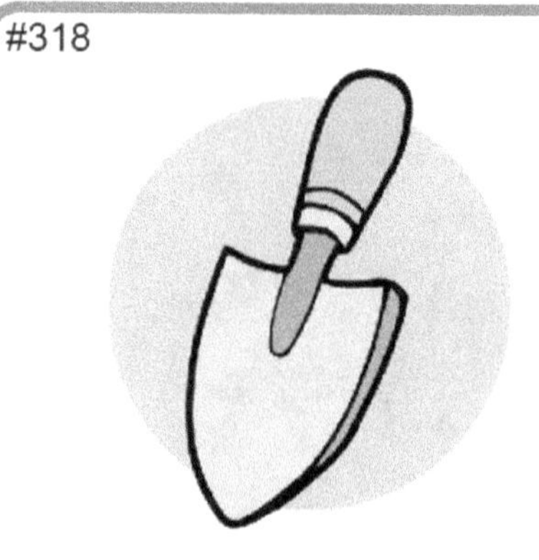

shovel

pelle

بیل

#319

calculator

calculatrice

ماشین‌حساب

#320

skirt

jupe

دامن

#321

pearls

perles

مروارید

#322

eraser

gomme

پاک‌کن

#323

bin

poubelle

سطل زباله

#324

television

télévision

تلویزیون

#325

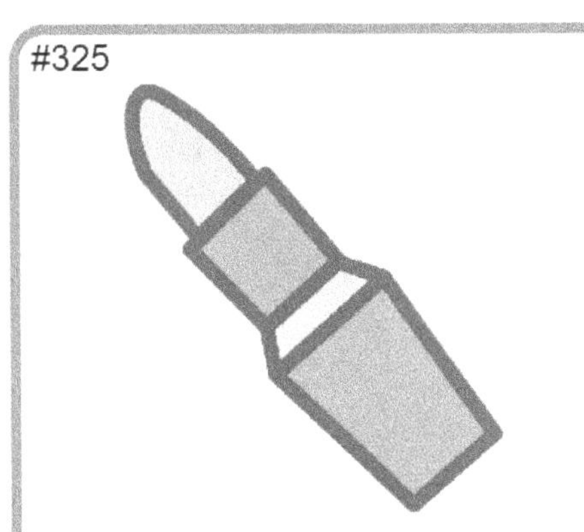

lipstick

rouge à lèvres

رژ لب

#326

torch

torche

مشعل

#327

bowtie

nœud papillon

پاپیون

#328

bed

lit

تخت

#329

ink

encre

جوهر

#330

carpet

tapis

فرش

#331

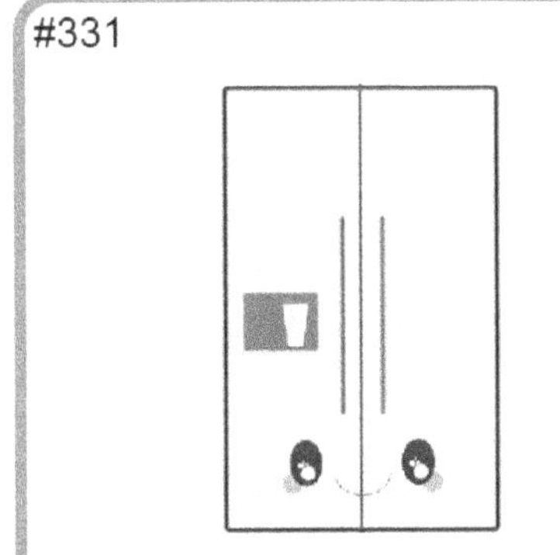

refrigerator

réfrigérateur

یخچال

#332

jacket

veste

ژاکت

#333

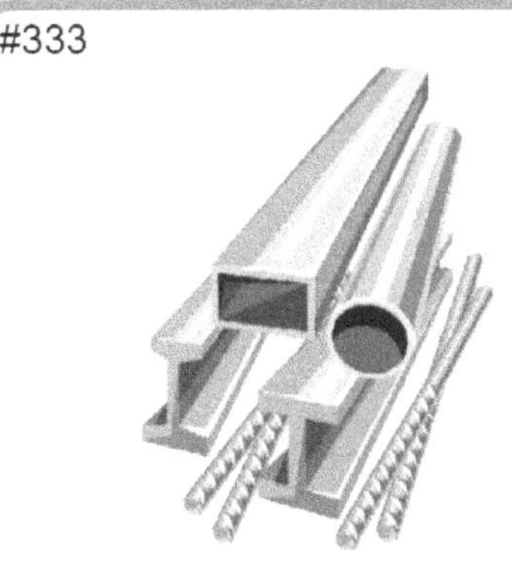

metal

métal

فلز

#334

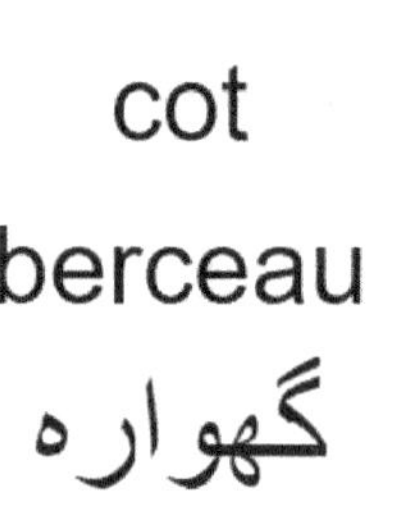

cot

berceau

گهواره

#335

kettle

bouilloire

کتری

#336

scissors

ciseaux

قیچی

#337

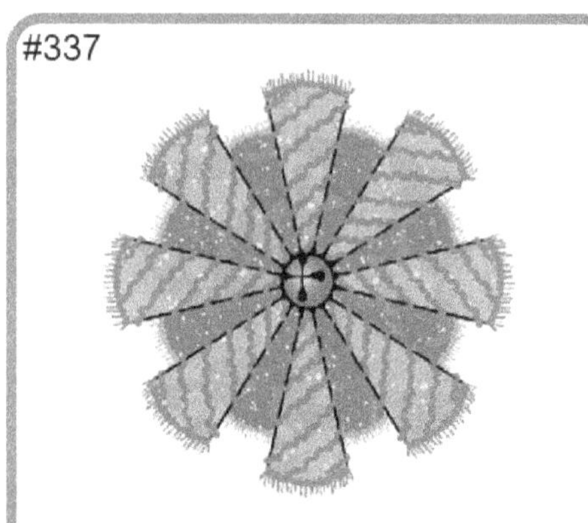

wreath

couronne

تاج گل

#338

ladder

échelle

نردبان

#339

cap

casquette

کلاه

#340

paper

papier

کاغذ

#341

bouquet

bouquet

دسته گل

#342

seeds

graines

بذر

#343

napkin

serviette

دستمال

#344

notebook

cahier

دفترچه

#345

necklace

collier

گردنبند

#346

bottle

bouteille

بطری

#347

belt

ceinture

کمربند

#348

desk

bureau

میز

#349

cash

argent liquide

پول نقد

#350

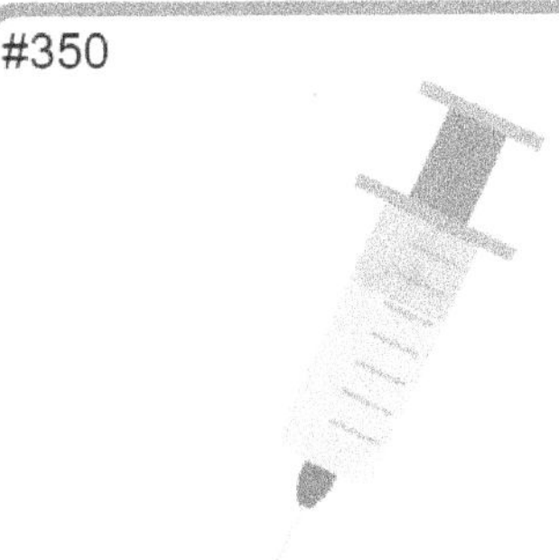

syringe

seringue

سرنگ

#351

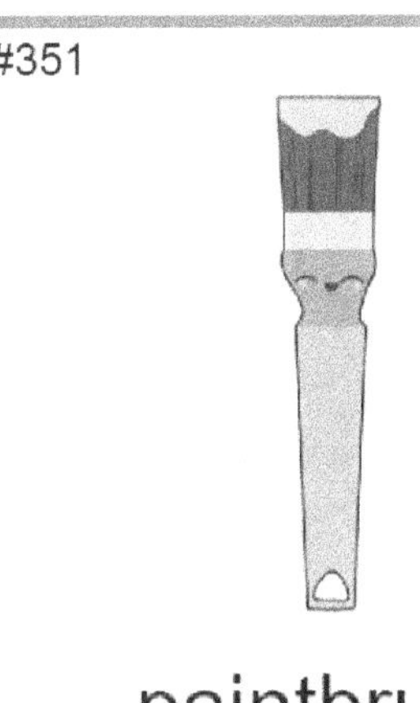

paintbrush

pinceau

قلممو

#352

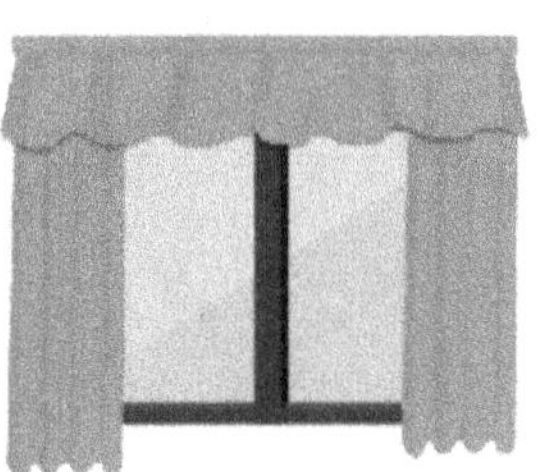

curtains

rideaux

پرده‌ها

#353

pitcher

carafe

پارچ

#354

wallet

portefeuille

کیف پول

#355

bookcase

bibliothèque

قفسه کتاب

#356

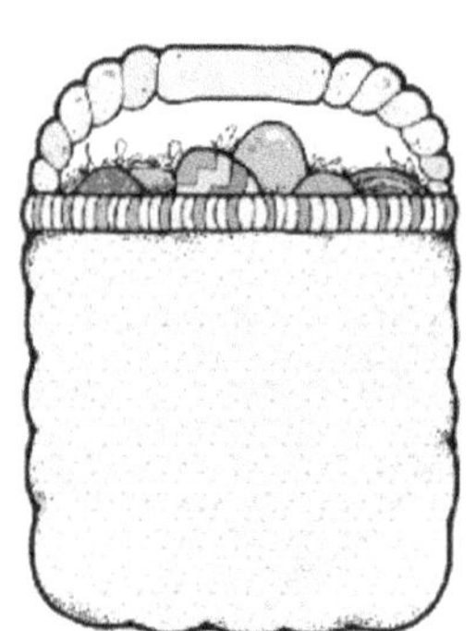

basket

panier

سبد

#357

spatula

spatule

کفگیر

#358

crayons

crayons

مداد شمعی

#359

undershirt

débardeur

زیرپوش

#360

apron

tablier

پیشبند

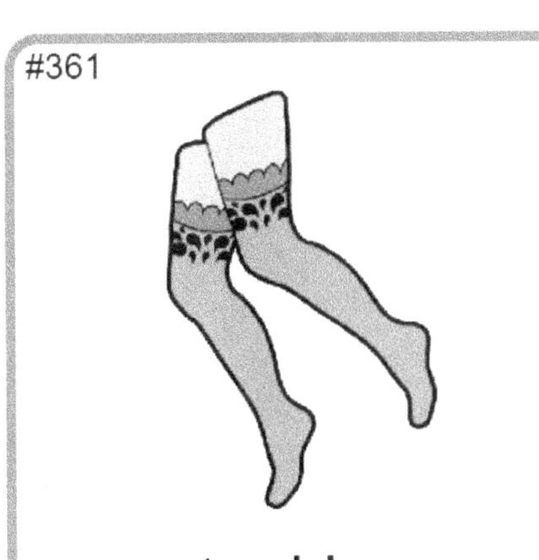

#361

stockings

bas

جوراب شلواری

#362

pan

poêle

ماهیتابه

#363

bowl

bol

کاسه

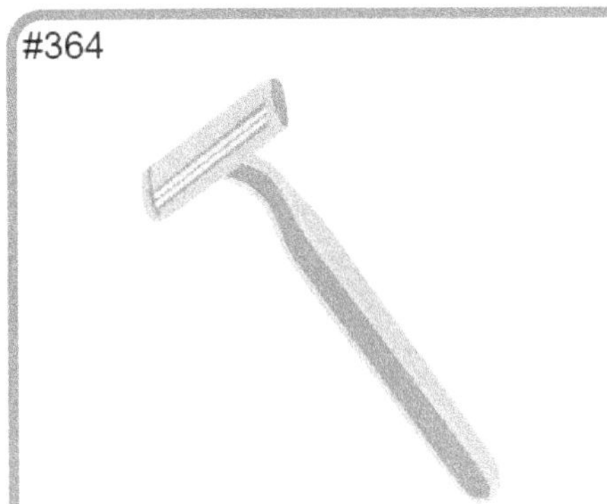

#364

razor

rasoir

تیغ

#365

tire

pneu

لاستیک

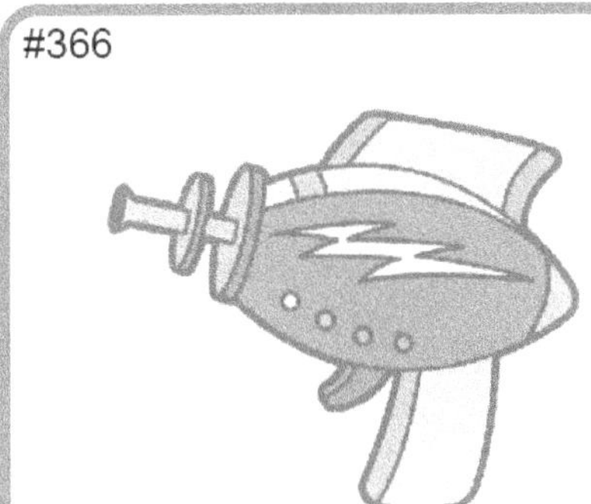

#366

gun

pistolet

تفنگ

#367

saucer

soucoupe

نعلبکی

#368

cage

cage

قفس

#369

flag

drapeau

پرچم

#370

pacifier

sucette

پستانک

#371

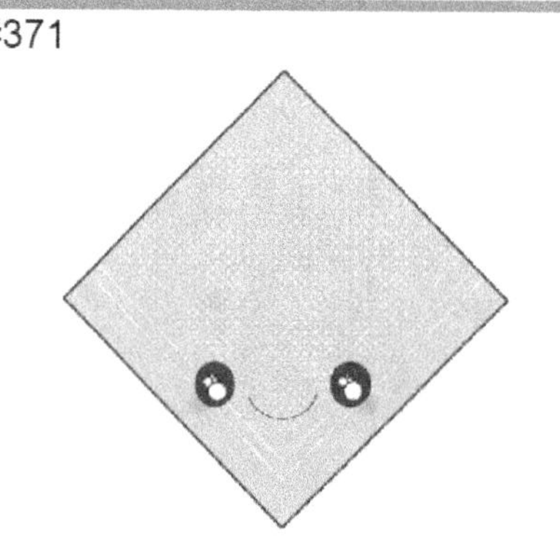

handkerchief

mouchoir

دستمال جیبی

#372

rope

corde

طناب

#373

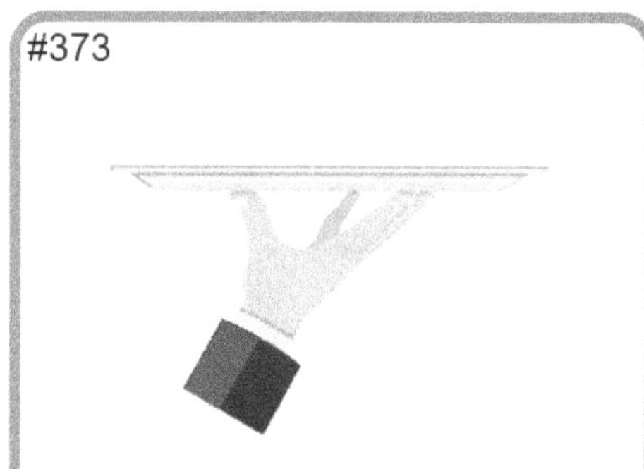

tray

plateau

سینی

#374

bucket

seau

سطل

#375

toothbrush

brosse à dents

مسواک

#376

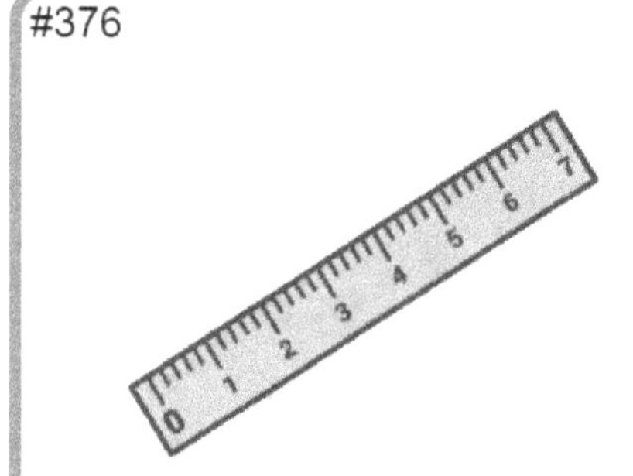

ruler

règle

خطکش

#377

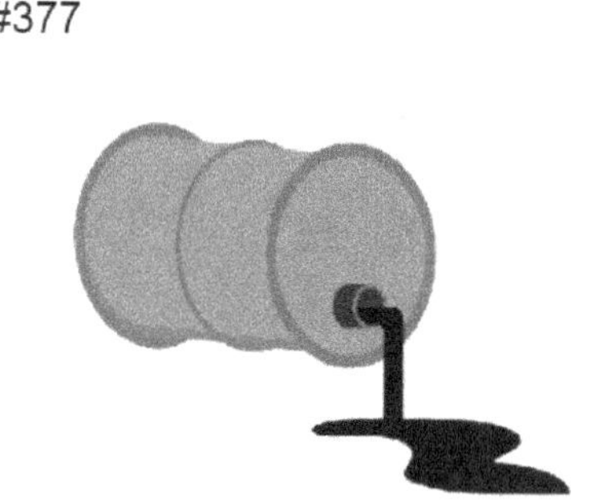

oil

huile

روغن

#378

scarf

écharpe

شال

#379

fork

fourchette

چنگال

#380

chalkboard

tableau noir

تخته سیاه

#381

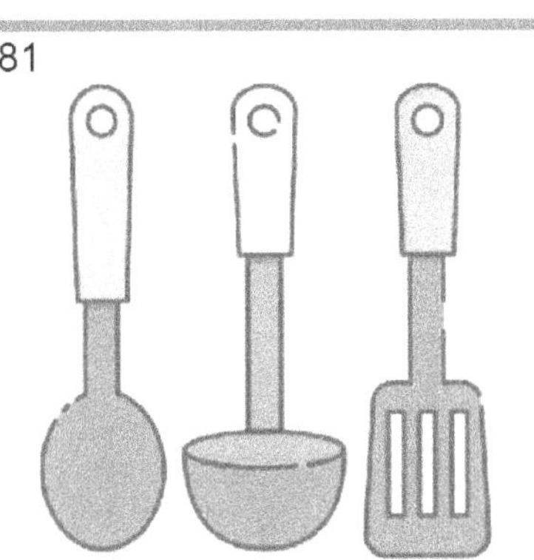

utensils

ustensiles

ظروف آشپزخانه

#382

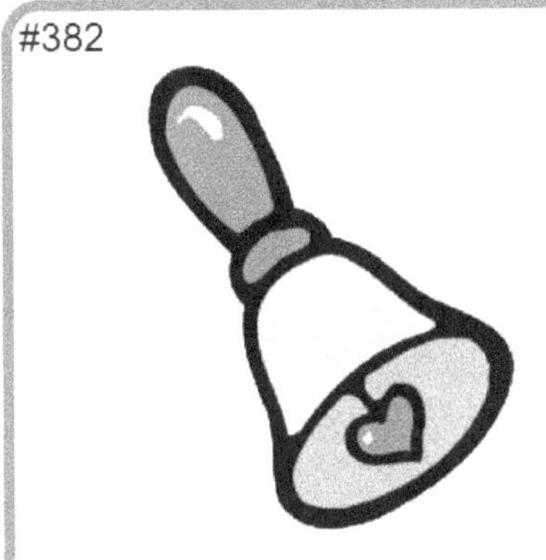

bell

cloche

زنگ

#383

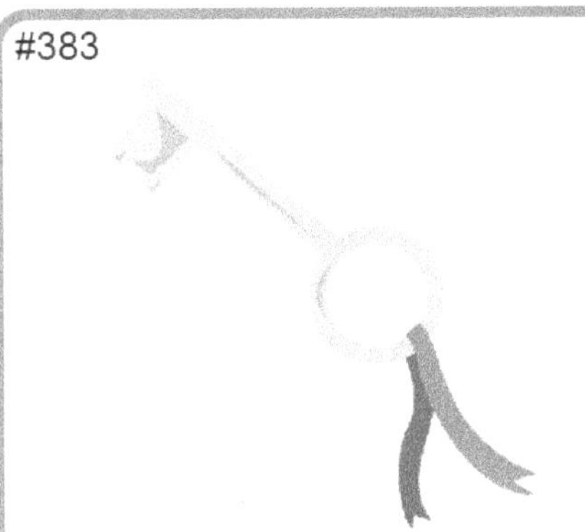

key

clé

کلید

#384

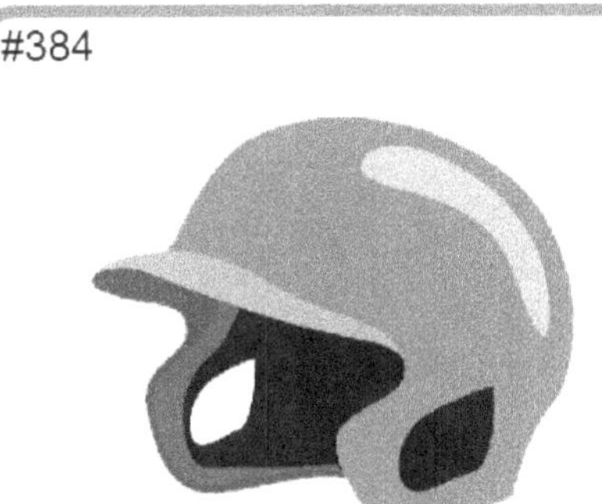

helmet

casque

کلاه ایمنی

#385

rake

râteau

چنگک

#386

tool

outil

ابزار

#387

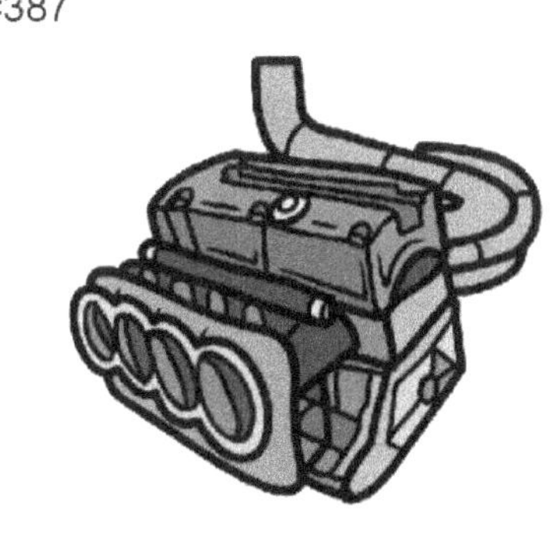

engine

moteur

موتور

#388

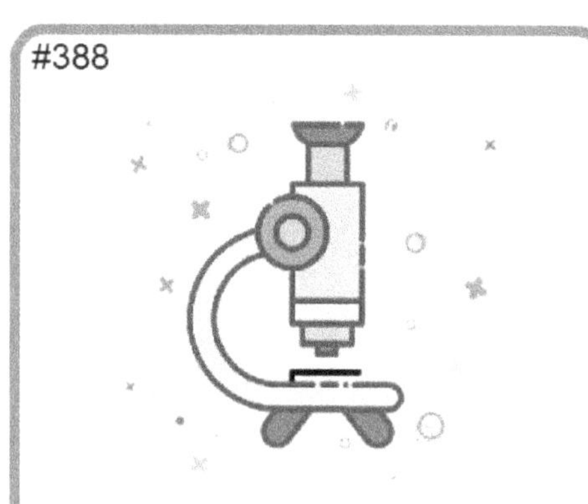

microscope

microscope

میکروسکوپ

#389

prize

prix

جایزه

#390

money

argent

پول

#391

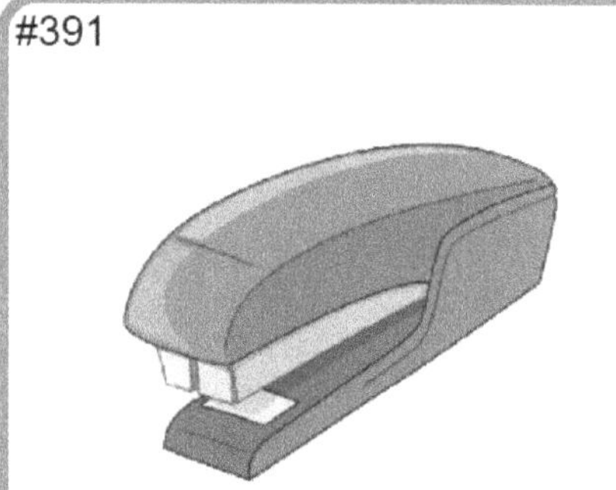

stapler

agrafeuse

منگنه

#392

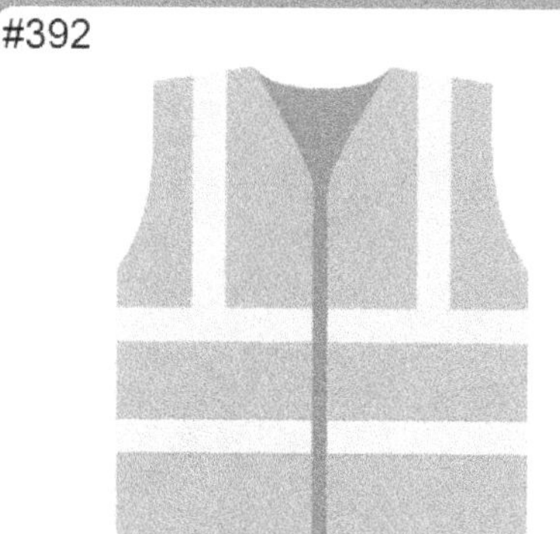

vest

gilet

جلیقه

#393

tent

tente

چادر

#394

doll

poupée

عروسک

#395

calendar

calendrier

تقویم

#396

backpack

sac à dos

کوله‌پشتی

#397

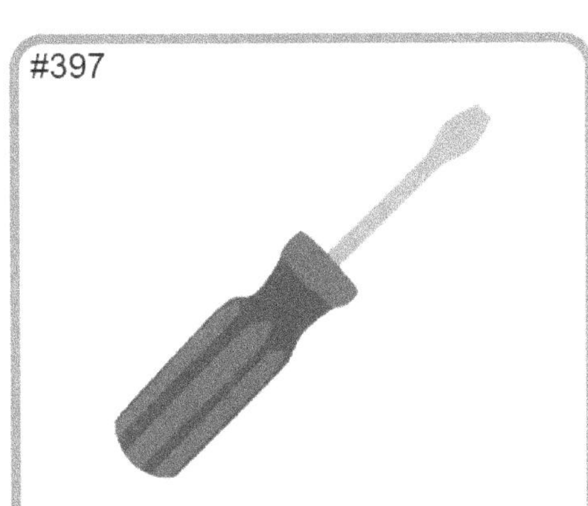

screwdriver

tournevis

پیچ‌گوشتی

#398

equipment

équipement

تجهیزات

#399

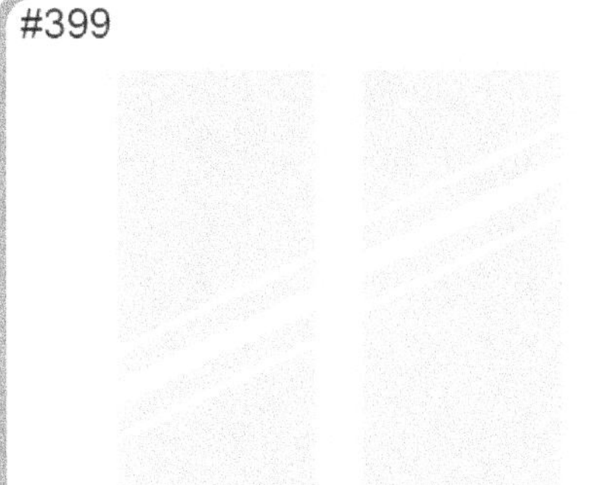

glass

verre

شیشه

#400

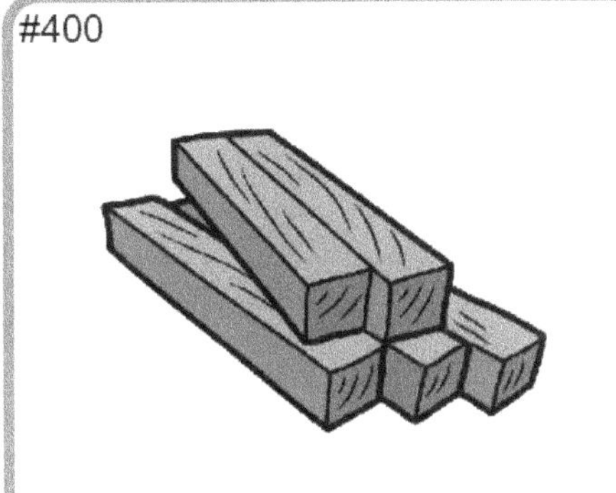

wood

bois

چوب

#401

gift

cadeau

هدیه

#402

umbrella

parapluie

چتر

#403

clock

horloge

ساعت

#404

crayon

crayon

مداد شمعی

#405

camera

appareil photo

دوربین

#406

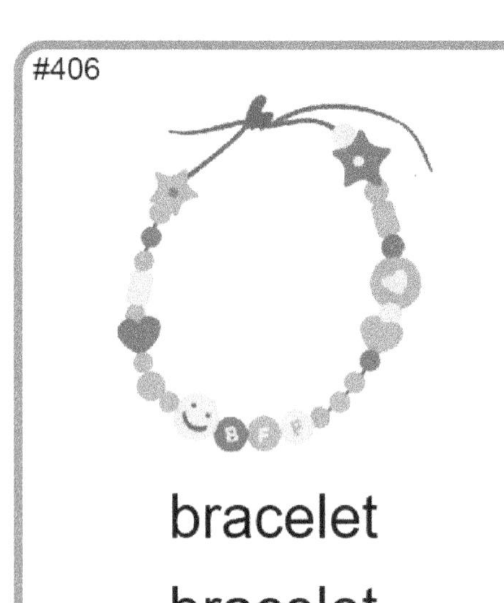

bracelet

bracelet

دستبند

#407

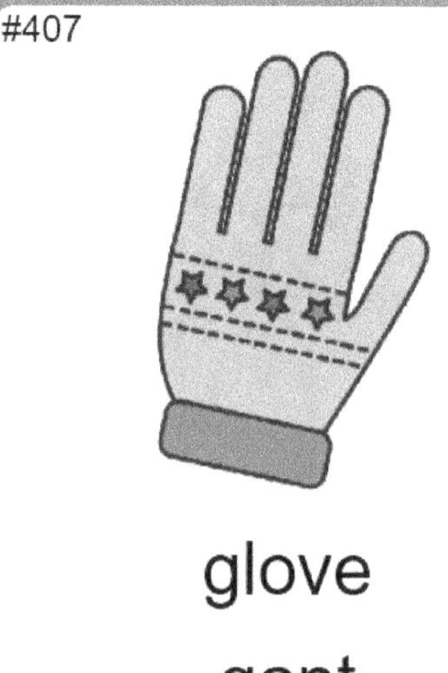

glove

gant

دستکش

#408

mud

boue

گل و لای

#409

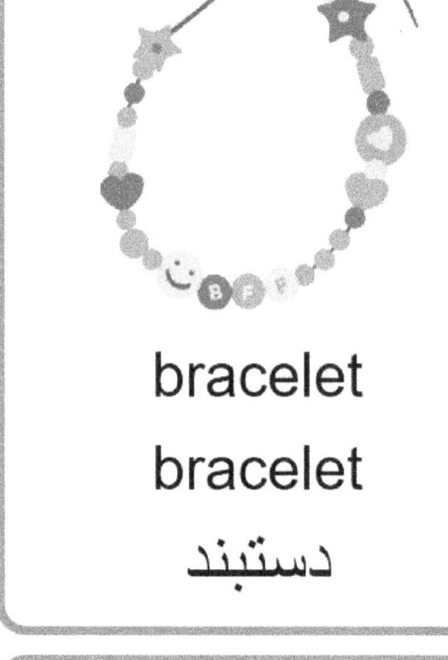

shower

douche

دوش گرفتن

#410

tree

arbre

درخت

#411

stone

pierre

سنگ

#412

ground

sol

زمین

#413

street

rue

خیابان

#414

garden

jardin

باغ

#415

puddle

flaque

گودال

#416

tombstone

pierre tombale

سنگ قبر

#417

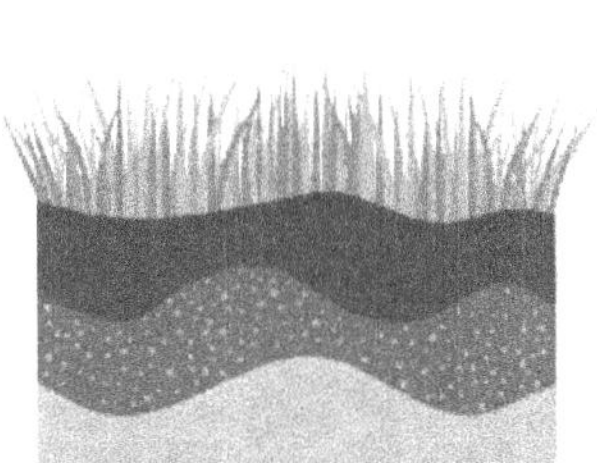

soil

sol

خاک

#418

chimney

cheminée

دودکش

#419

clothesline

corde à linge

بند رخت

#420

house

maison

خانه

#421

sinks

éviers

سینک‌ها

#422

hall

salle

سالن

#423

office

bureau

دفتر

#424

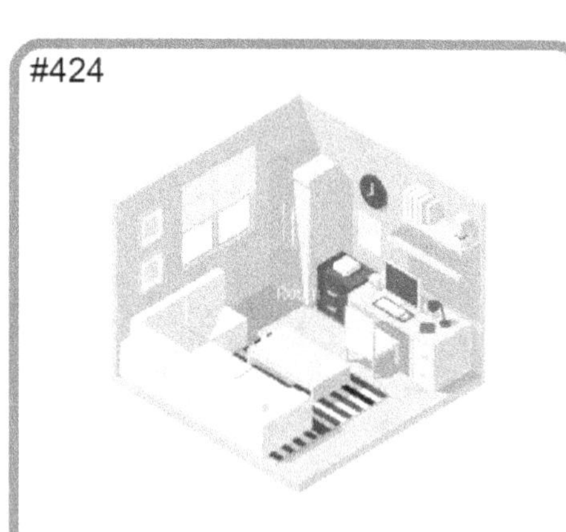

room

chambre

اتاق

#425

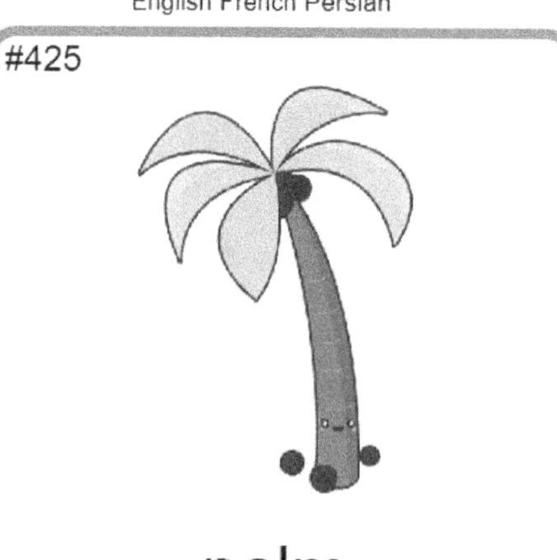

palm

palmier

نخل

#426

farm

ferme

مزرعه

#427

grass

herbe

چمن

#428

area

zone

منطقه

#429

wall

mur

دیوار

#430

shelter

abri

پناهگاه

#431

dust

poussière

گرد و غبار

#432

bridge

pont

پل

#433

brick

brique

آجر

#434

flower

fleur

گل

#435

road

route

جاده

#436

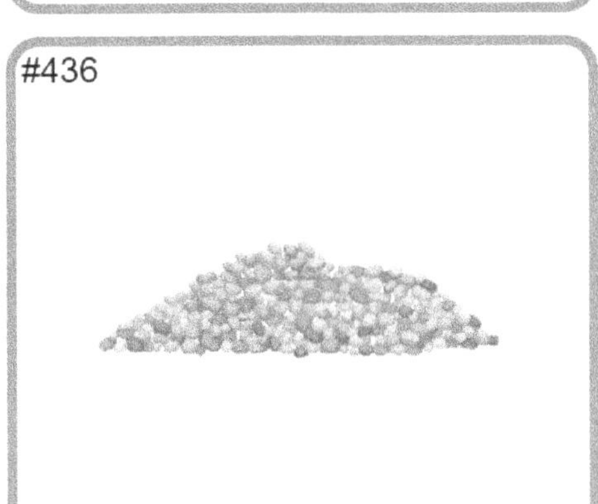

gravel

gravier

شن

#437

home

maison

خانه

#438

hut

cabane

کلبه

#439

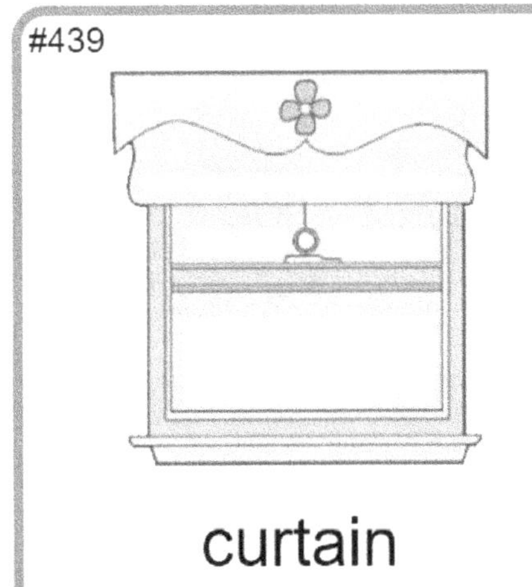
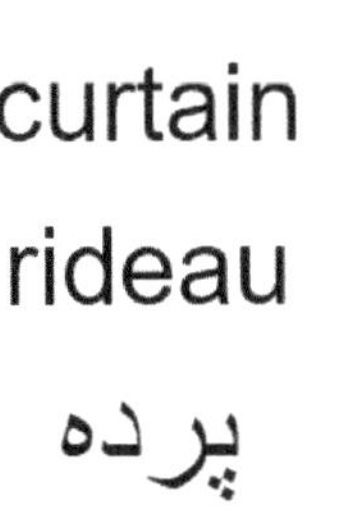

curtain

rideau

پرده

#440

windmill

moulin à vent

آسیاب بادی

#441

garbage

ordures

زباله

#442

door

porte

در

#443

pool

piscine

استخر

#444

faucet

robinet

شیر آب

#445

rock

roche

سنگ

#446

fence

clôture

حصار

#447

castle

château

قلعه

#448

building

bâtiment

ساختمان

#449

field

champ

مزرعه

#450

bathroom

salle de bain

حمام

#451

leaf

feuille

برگ

#452

roof

toit

سقف

#453

trash

déchets

زباله

#454

gate

porte

دروازه

#455

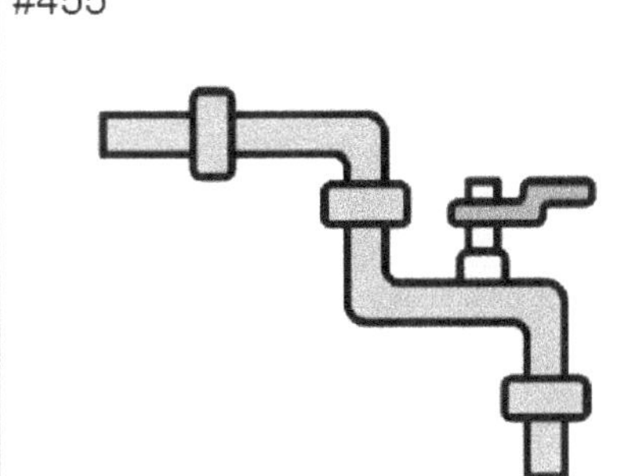

pipe

tuyau

لوله

#456

think

penser

فکر کردن

#457

wash

laver

شستن

#458

prepare

préparer

آماده کردن

#459

choose

choisir

انتخاب کردن

#460

read

lire

خواندن

#461

decrease

diminuer

کاهش

#462

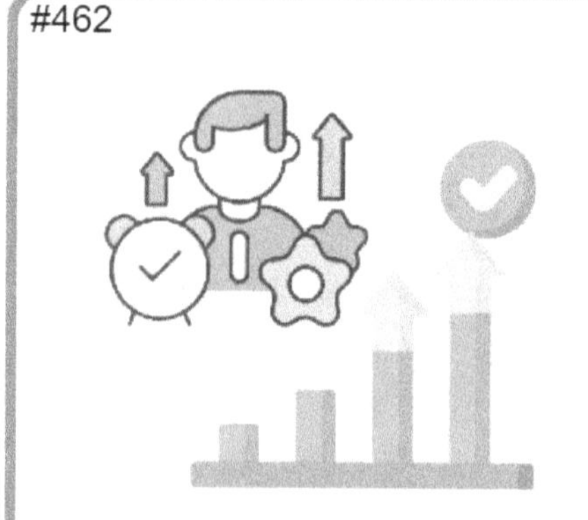

improve

améliorer

بهبود بخشیدن

#463

talk

parler

صحبت کردن

#464

write

écrire

نوشتن

#465

sleep

dormir

خوابیدن

#466

close

fermer

بستن

#467

protect

protéger

محافظت کردن

#468

avoid

éviter

اجتناب کردن

#469

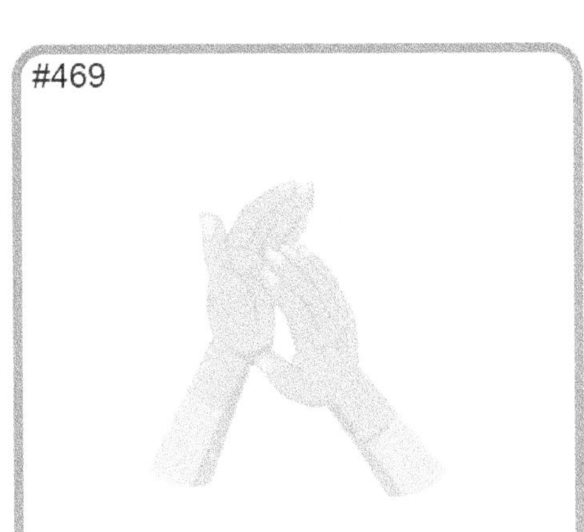

clap

applaudir

دست زدن

#470

listen

écouter

گوش دادن

#471

dig

creuser

حفاری

#472

grill

griller

کباب کردن

#473

play

jouer

بازی کردن

#474

dream

rêver

رویا دیدن

#475

love

aimer

عشق

#476

drink

boire

نوشیدن

#477

believe

croire

باور کردن

#478

race

course

مسابقه

#479

sing

chanter

آواز خواندن

#480

fly

voler

پرواز

#481

run

courir

دویدن

#482

eat

manger

خوردن

#483

hug

câlin

بغل کردن

#484

understand

comprendre

فهمیدن

#485

wait

attendre

صبر کردن

#486

stop

arrêter

توقف

#487

solve

résoudre

حل کردن

#488

smile

sourire

لبخند

#489

prevent

prévenir

جلوگیری کردن

#490

laugh

rire

خندیدن

#491

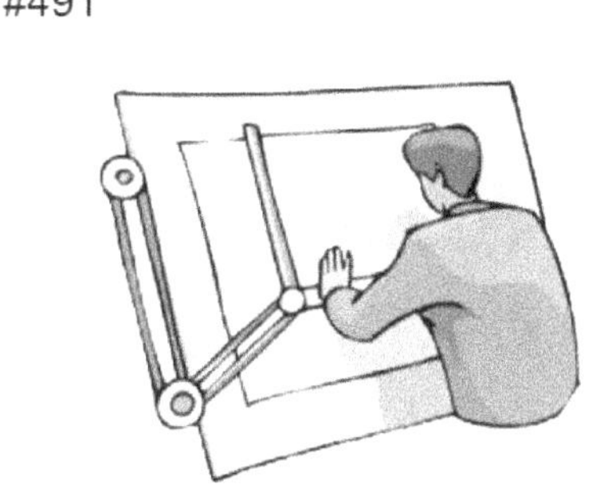

sketch

esquisse

طرح

#492

grow

grandir

رشد کردن

#493

fry

frire

سرخ کردن

#494

discover

découvrir

کشف کردن

#495

bite

mordre

گاز گرفتن

#496

bathe

se baigner

حمام کردن

#497

create

créer

خلق کردن

#498

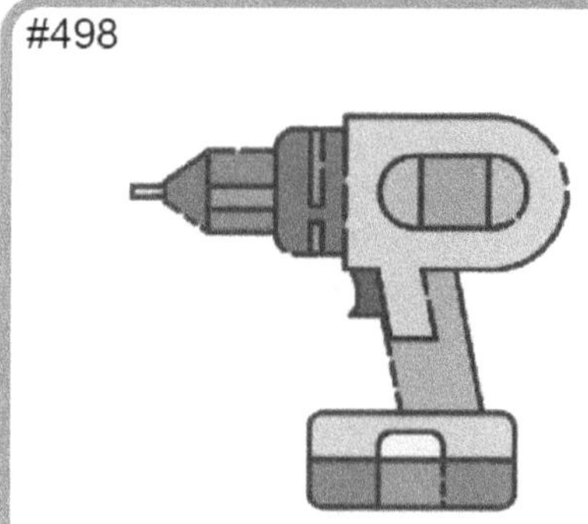

drill

percer

مته

#499

angry

en colère

عصبانی

#500

remember

se souvenir

به خاطر سپردن

#501

help

aider

کمک کردن

#502

beg

mendier

التماس کردن

#503

speak

parler

صحبت کردن

#504

shake

secouer

تکان دادن

#505

roast

rôti

کباب کردن

#506

walk

marcher

راه رفتن

#507

achieve

atteindre

دستیابی

#508

thank

remercier

تشکر

#509

tame

apprivoiser

اهلی کردن

#510

follow

suivre

دنبال کردن

#511

cut

couper

بریدن

#512

prefer

préférer

ترجیح دادن

#513

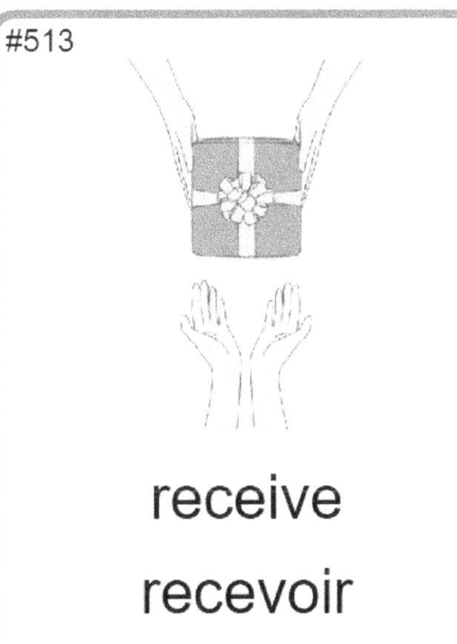

receive

recevoir

دریافت کردن

#514

nap

sieste

چرت زدن

#515

wag

remuer

تکان دادن

#516

invest

investir

سرمایه‌گذاری

#517

hide

cacher

پنهان کردن

#518

meet

rencontrer

ملاقات کردن

#519

nibble

grignoter

نیش زدن

#520

develop

développer

توسعه دادن

#521

teach

enseigner

تدریس کردن

#522

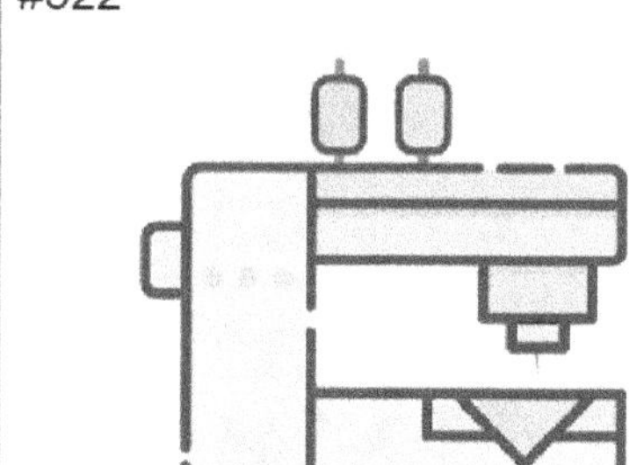

sew

coudre

دوختن

#523

hurt

blesser

آسیب دیدن

#524

come

venir

آمدن

#525

cry

pleurer

گریه کردن

#526

bake

cuire

پختن

#527

build

construire

ساختن

#528

goodbye

au revoir

خداحافظ

#529

cook

cuisiner

پختن

#530

open

ouvrir

باز کردن

#531

rob

voler

دزدیدن

#532

sit

s'asseoir

نشستن

#533

clean

nettoyer

تمیز کردن

#534

smell

odeur

بو

#535

forbid

interdire

ممنوع کردن

#536

snore

ronfler

خرناس کشیدن

#537

crawl

ramper

خزیدن

#538

jump

sauter

پرش

#539

win

gagner

برنده شدن

#540

buy

acheter

خریدن

#541	#542	#543

enjoy

apprécier

لذت بردن

respect

respect

احترام گذاشتن

boil

bouillir

جوشاندن

#544	#545	#546

hello

bonjour

سلام

celebrate

célébrer

جشن گرفتن

climb

grimper

بالا رفتن

#547	#548	#549

sick

malade

بیمار

kiss

embrasser

بوسه

discuss

discuter

بحث کردن

#550

give

donner

دادن

#551

knit

tricoter

بافتن

#552

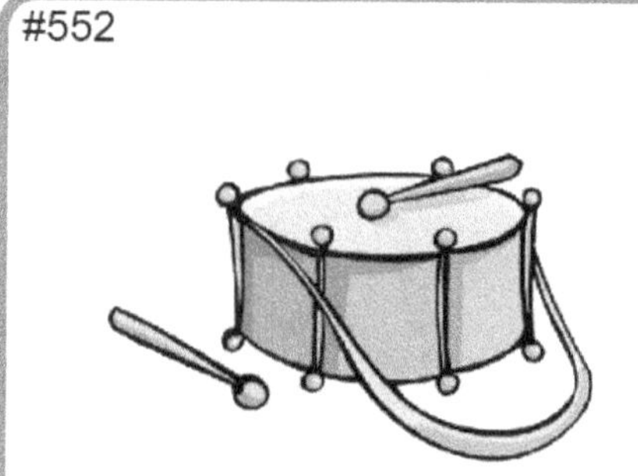

drum

tambour

طبل

#553

violin

violon

ویولن

#554

piano

piano

پیانو

#555

guitar

guitare

گیتار

#556

music

musique

موسیقی

#557

zero

zéro

صفر

#558

one

un

یکی

#559

two

deux

دو

#560

three

trois

سه

#561

four

quatre

چهار

#562

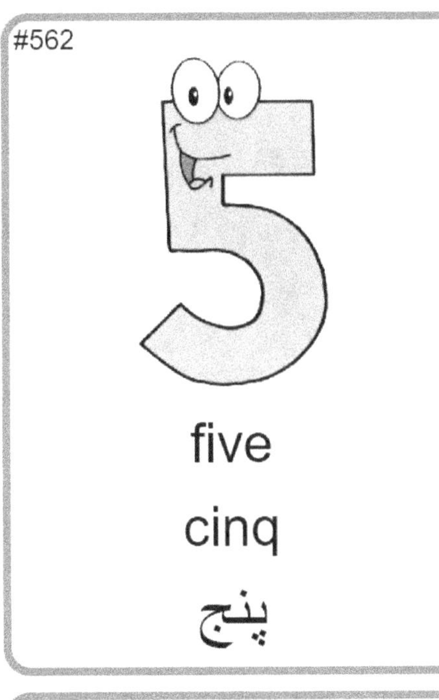

five

cinq

پنج

#563

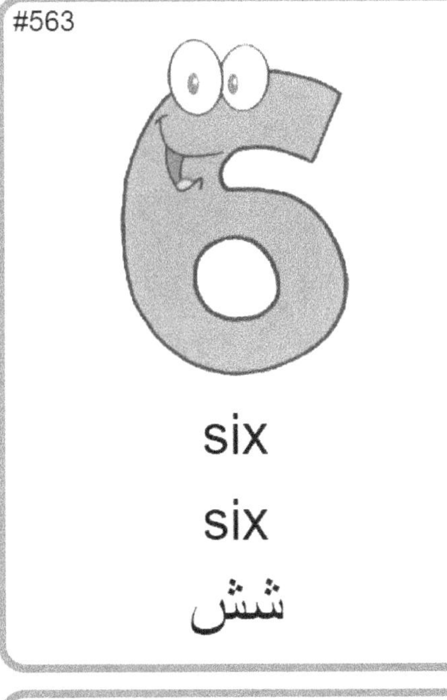

six

six

شش

#564

seven

sept

هفت

#565

eight

huit

هشت

#566

nine

neuf

نه

#567

ten

dix

ده

#568

eleven

onze

یازده

#569

twelve

douze

دوازده

#570

thirteen

treize

سیزده

#571

fourteen

quatorze

چهارده

#572

fifteen

quinze

پانزده

#573

sixteen

seize

شانزده

#574

seventeen

dix-sept

هفده

#575

eighteen

dix-huit

هجده

#576

nineteen

dix-neuf

نوزده

#577

twenty

vingt

بیست

#578

twenty one

vingt et un

بیست و یک

#579

twenty two

vingt-deux

بیست و دو

#580

twenty three

vingt-trois

بیست و سه

#581

twenty four

vingt-quatre

بیست و چهار

#582

twenty five

vingt-cinq

بیست و پنج

#583

twenty six

vingt-six

بیست و شش

#584

twenty seven

vingt-sept

بیست و هفت

#585

twenty eight

vingt-huit

بیست و هشت

#586

29

twenty nine

vingt-neuf

بیست و نه

#587

30

thirty

trente

سی

#588

31

thirty one

trente-et-un

سی و یک

#589

32

thirty two

trente-deux

سی و دو

#590

33

thirty three

trente-trois

سی و سه

#591

34

thirty four

trente-quatre

سی و چهار

#592

35

thirty five

trente-cinq

سی و پنج

#593

36

thirty six

trente-six

سی و شش

#594

37

thirty seven

trente-sept

سی و هفت

#595

38 

thirty eight

trente-huit

سی و هشت

#596

39 

thirty nine

trente-neuf

سی و نه

#597

40

forty

quarante

چهل

#598

41 

forty one

quarante et un

چهل و یک

#599

42 

forty two

quarante-deux

چهل و دو

#600

43

forty three

quarante-trois

چهل و سه

#601

44 

forty four

quarante-quatre

چهل و چهار

#602

45 

forty five

quarante-cinq

چهل و پنج

#603

46

forty six

quarante-six

چهل و شش

#604

47

forty seven

quarante-sept

چهل و هفت

#605

48

forty eight

quarante-huit

چهل و هشت

#606

49

forty nine

quarante-neuf

چهل و نه

#607

50

fifty

cinquante

پنجاه

#608

51

fifty one

cinquante et un

پنجاه و یک

#609

52

fifty two

cinquante-deux

پنجاه و دو

#610

53

fifty three

cinquante-trois

پنجاه و سه

#611

54

fifty four

cinquante-quatre

پنجاه و چهار

#612

55

fifty five

cinquante-cinq

پنجاه و پنج

#613
56
fifty six
cinquante-six
پنجاه و شش

#614
57

fifty seven
cinquante-sept
پنجاه و هفت

#615
58

fifty eight
cinquante-huit
پنجاه و هشت

#616
59
fifty nine
cinquante-neuf
پنجاه و نه

#617
60
sixty
soixante
شصت

#618
61
sixty one
soixante et un
شصت و یک

#619
62
sixty two
soixante-deux
شصت و دو

#620
63
sixty three
soixante-trois
شصت و سه

#621
64
sixty four
soixante-quatre
شصت و چهار

#622

65

sixty five

soixante-cinq

شصت و پنج

#623

66

sixty six

soixante-six

شصت و شش

#624

67

sixty seven

soixante-sept

شصت و هفت

#625

68

sixty eight

soixante-huit

شصت و هشت

#626

69

sixty nine

soixante-neuf

شصت و نه

#627

70

seventy

soixante-dix

هفتاد

#628

71

seventy one

soixante et onze

هفتاد و یک

#629

72

seventy two

soixante-douze

هفتاد و دو

#630

73

seventy three

soixante-treize

هفتاد و سه

#631

74

seventy four

soixante-quatorze

هفتاد و چهار

#632

75

seventy five

soixante-quinze

هفتاد و پنج

#633

76

seventy six

soixante-seize

هفتاد و شش

#634

77

seventy seven

soixante-dix-sept

هفتاد و هفت

#635

78

seventy eight

soixante-dix-huit

هفتاد و هشت

#636

79

seventy nine

soixante-dix-neuf

هفتاد و نه

#637

80

eighty

quatre-vingts

هشتاد

#638

81

eighty one

quatre-vingt-un

هشتاد و یک

#639

82

eighty two

quatre-vingt-deux

هشتاد و دو

#640

83

eighty three

quatre-vingt-trois

هشتاد و سه

#641

84

eighty four

quatre-vingt-quatre

هشتاد و چهار

#642

85

eighty five

quatre-vingt-cinq

هشتاد و پنج

#643

86

eighty six

quatre-vingt-six

هشتاد و شش

#644

87

eighty seven

quatre-vingt-sept

هشتاد و هفت

#645

88

eighty eight

quatre-vingt-huit

هشتاد و هشت

#646

89

eighty nine

quatre-vingt-neuf

هشتاد و نه

#647

90

ninety

quatre-vingt-dix

نود

#648

91

ninety one

quatre-vingt-onze

نود و یک

#649

92

ninety two

quatre-vingt-douze

نود و دو

#650

93

ninety three

quatre-vingt-treize

نود و سه

#651

94

ninety four

quatre-vingt-quatorze

نود و چهار

#652

95

ninety five

quatre-vingt-quinze

نود و پنج

#653

96

ninety six

quatre-vingt-seize

نود و شش

#654

97

ninety seven

quatre-vingt-dix-sept

نود و هفت

#655

98

ninety eight

quatre-vingt-dix-huit

نود و هشت

#656

99

ninety nine

quatre-vingt-dix-neuf

نود و نه

#657

100

hundred

cent

صد

#658

thousand
mille
هزار

#659
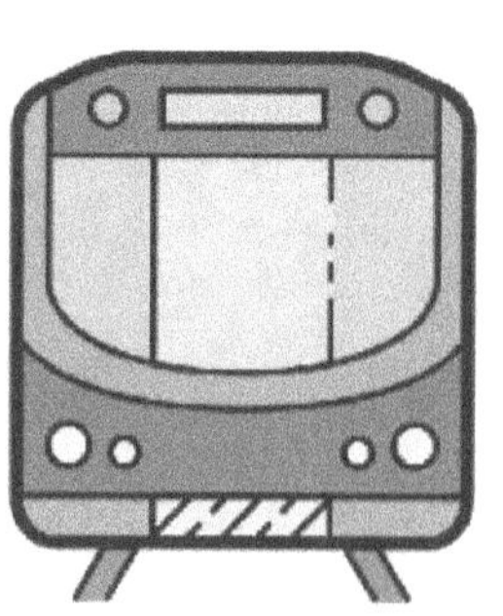
subway
métro
مترو

#660

submarine
sous-marin
زیردریایی

#661
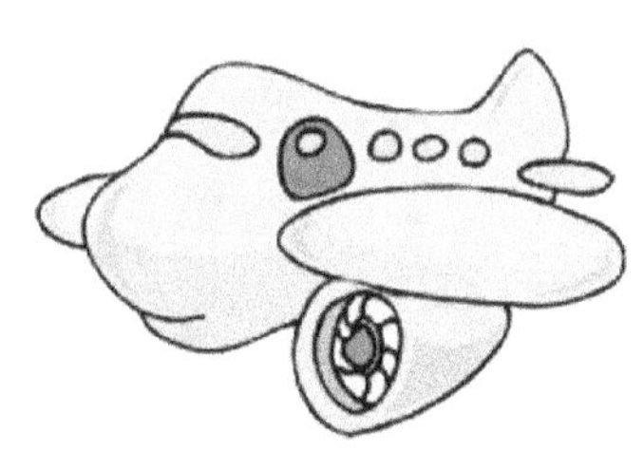
airplane
avion
هواپیما

#662

wagon
chariot
واگن

#663
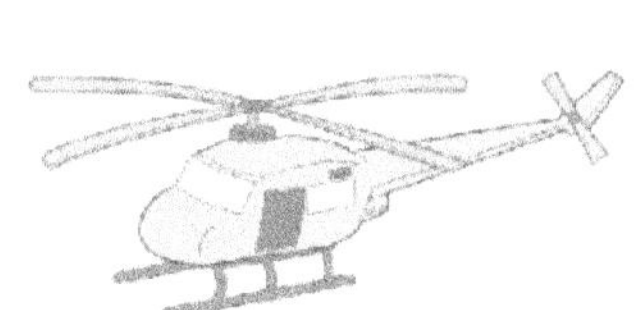
helicopter
hélicoptère
هلیکوپتر

#664

bicycle
vélo
دوچرخه

#665

car
voiture
ماشین

#666

plane
avion
هواپیما

#667

vehicle

véhicule

وسیله نقلیه

#668

scooter

scooter

اسکوتر

#669

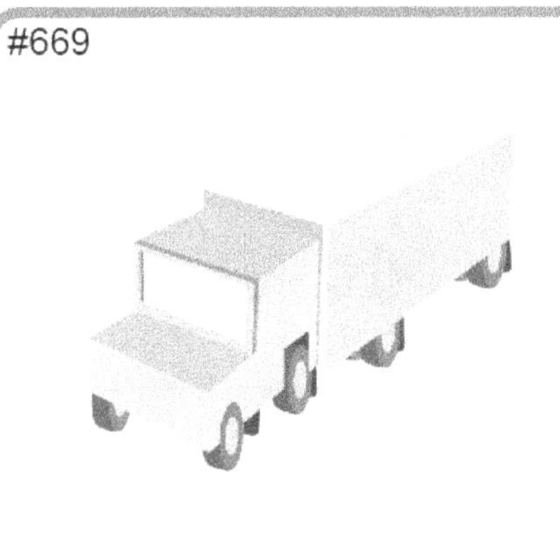

truck

camion

کامیون

#670

barrow

brouette

فرغون

#671

ship

navire

کشتی

#672

ferry

bac

کشتی مسافربری

#673

sailboat

voilier

قایق بادبانی

#674

boat

bateau

قایق

#675

motorcycle

moto

موتورسیکلت

#676

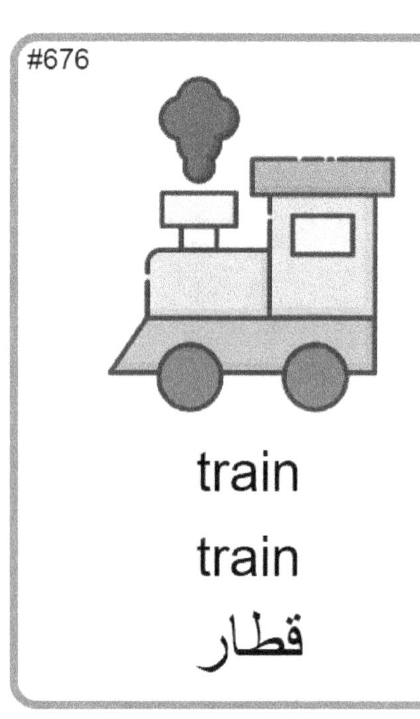

train
train
قطار

#677

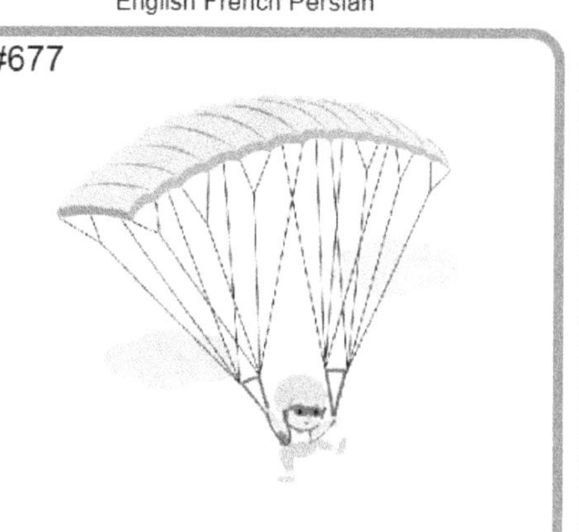

parachute
parachute
چتر نجات

#678

rocket
fusée
موشک

#679

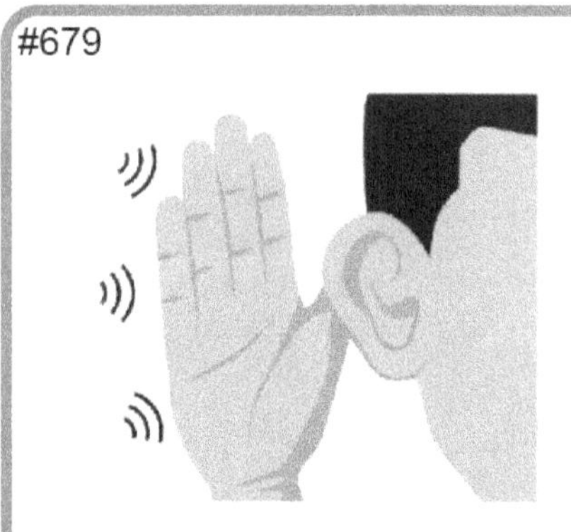

ear
oreille
گوش

#680

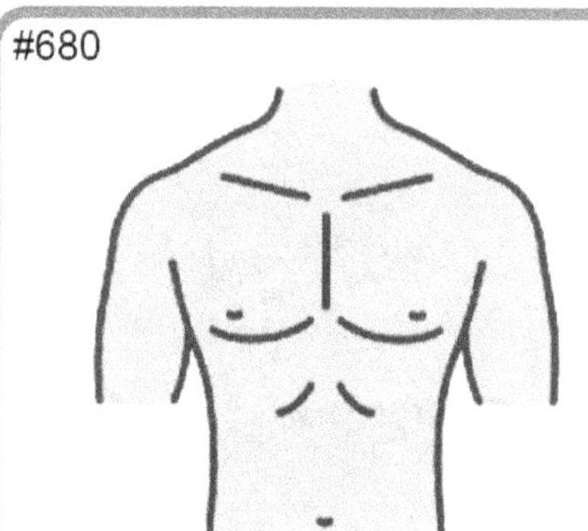

chest
poitrine
سینه

#681

shoulders
épaules
شانه‌ها

#682

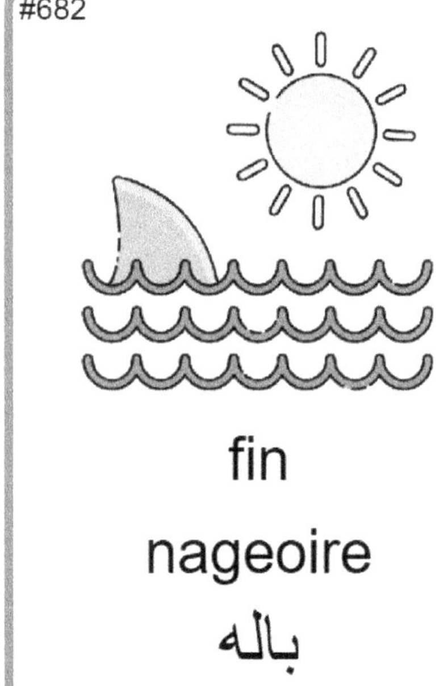

fin
nageoire
باله

#683

cheeks
joues
گونه‌ها

#684

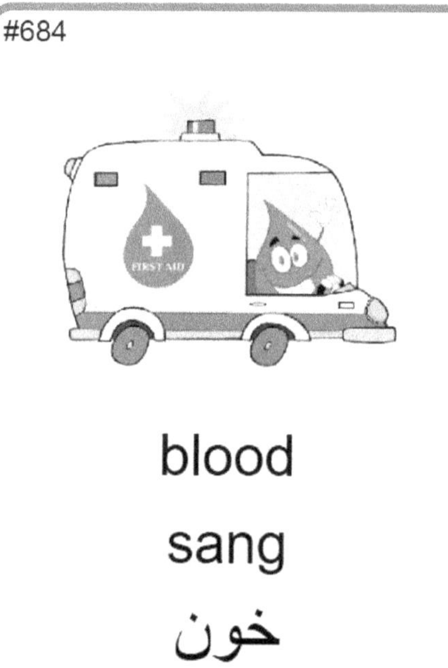

blood
sang
خون

#685

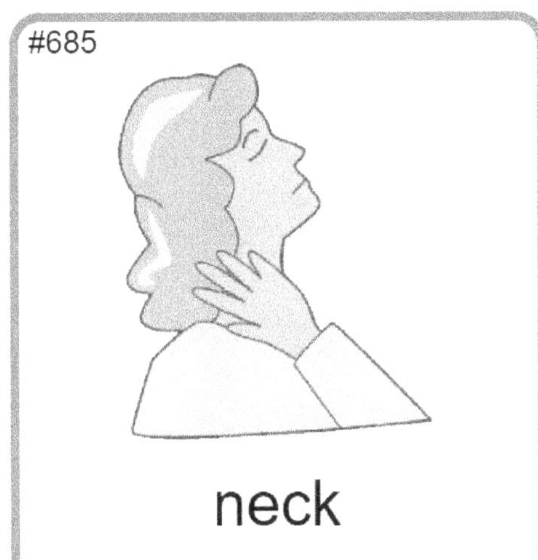

neck

cou

گردن

#686

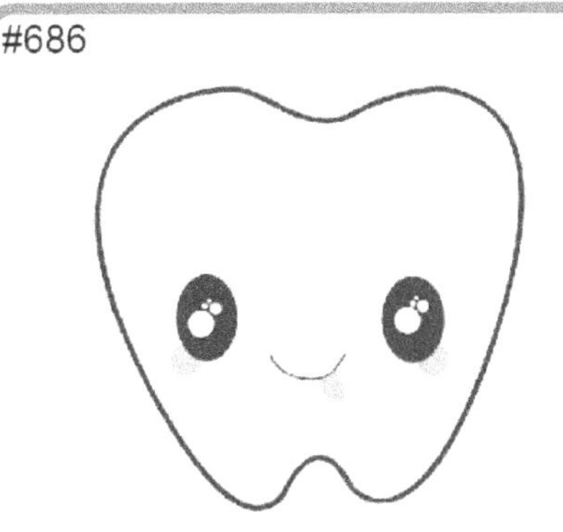

teeth

dents

دندان‌ها

#687

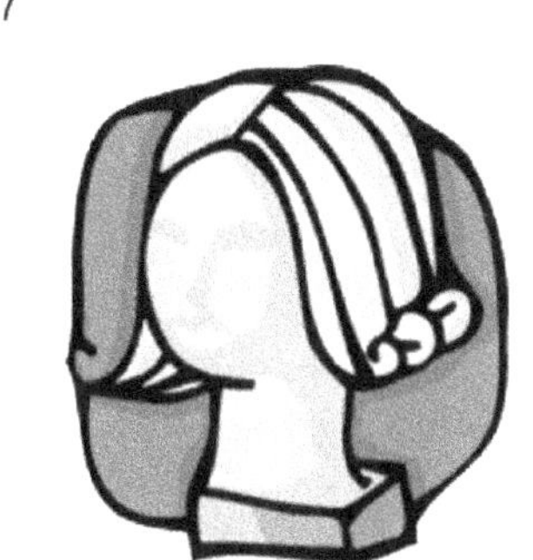

wig

perruque

کلاه‌گیس

#688

eye

œil

چشم

#689

knees

genoux

زانوها

#690

hair

cheveux

مو

#691

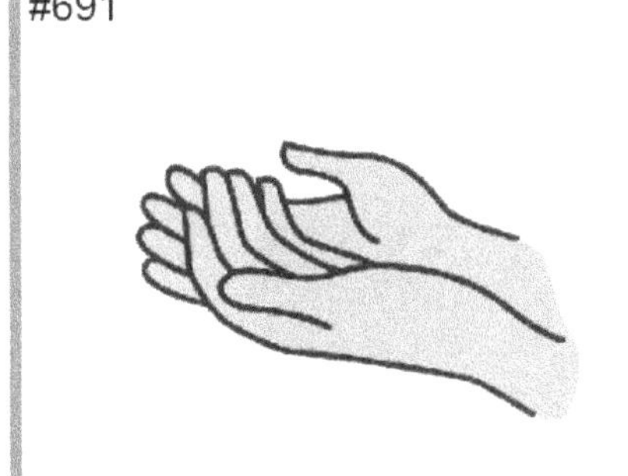

hands

mains

دست‌ها

#692

nose

nez

بینی

#693

brain

cerveau

مغز

#694

thumb

pouce

شست

#695

throat

gorge

گلو

#696

wing

aile

بال

#697

elbow

coude

آرنج

#698

tongue

langue

زبان

#699

foot

pied

پا

#700

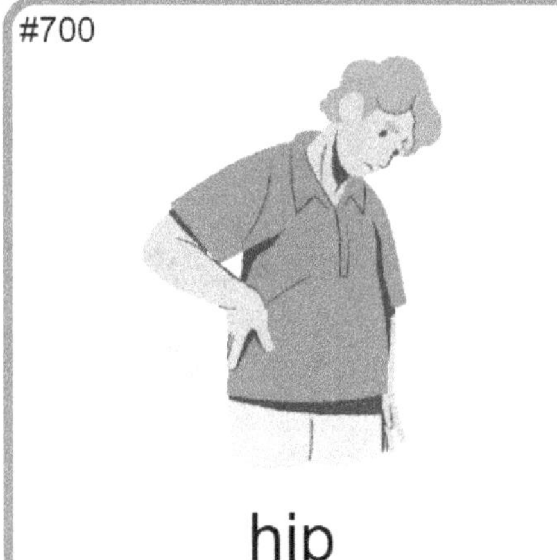

hip

hanche

لگن

#701

stomach

estomac

شکم

#702

body

corps

بدن

#703

heart

cœur

قلب

#704

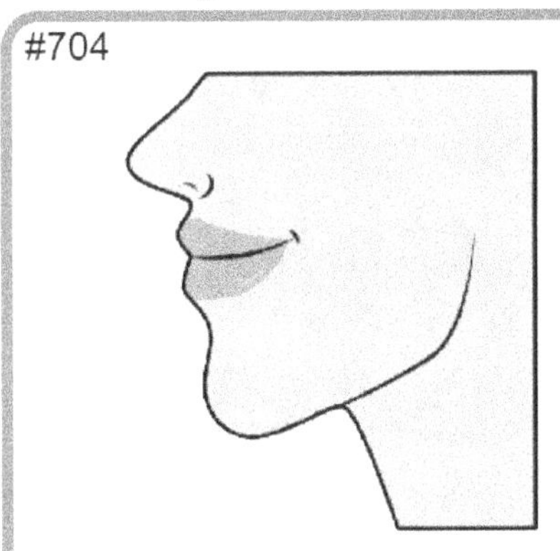

chin

menton

چانه

#705

eyebrows

sourcils

ابروها

#706

legs

jambes

پاها

#707

shoulder

épaule

شانه

#708

bone

os

استخوان

#709

waist

taille

کمر

#710

lips

lèvres

لب‌ها

#711

forehead

front

پیشانی

#712

beard

barbe

ریش

#713

face

visage

صورت

#714

glue

colle

چسب

#715

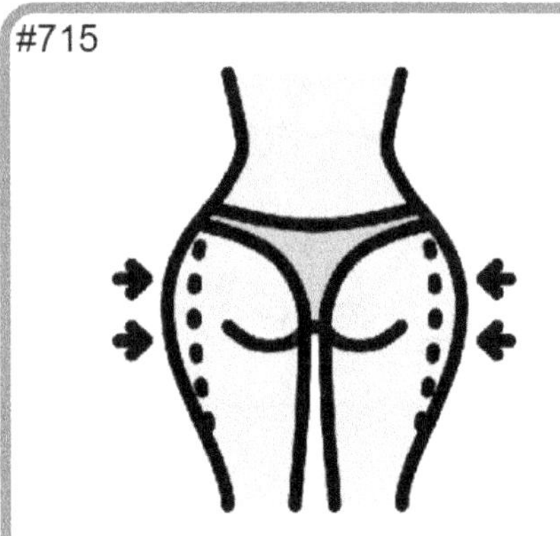

hips

hanches

لگن‌ها

#716

head

tête

سر

#717

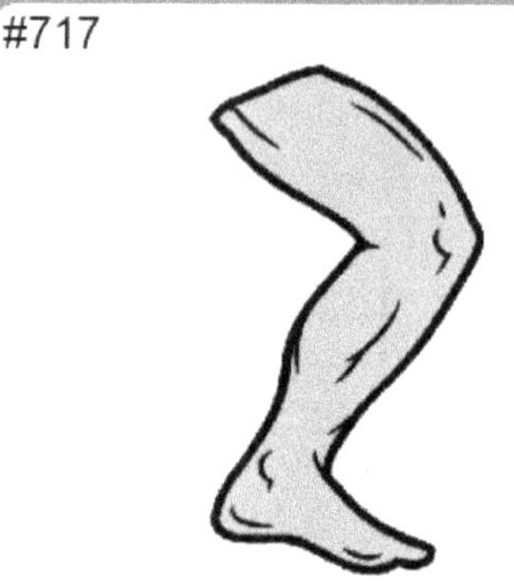

leg

jambe

پا

#718

tail

queue

دم

#719

muscle

muscle

ماهیچه

#720

toes

orteils

انگشتان پا

#721

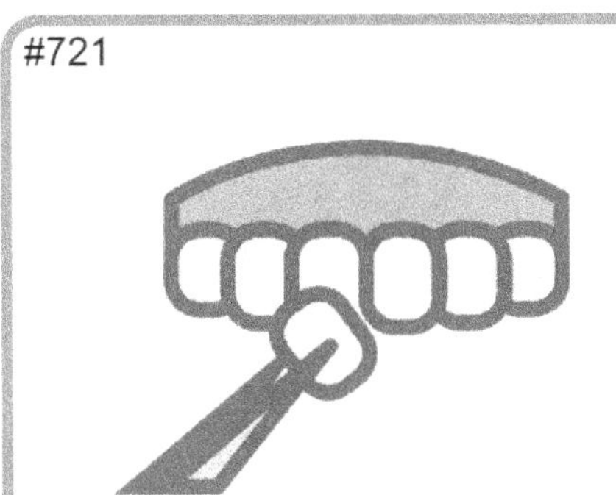

tooth

dent

دندان

#722

feet

pieds

پاها

#723

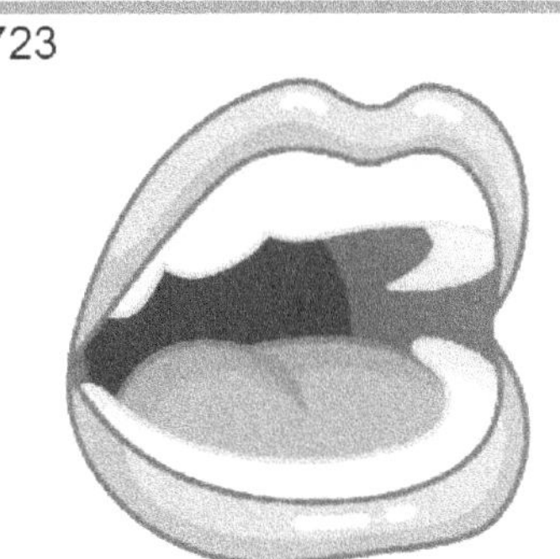

mouth

bouche

دهان

#724

driving

conduite

رانندگی

#725

archery

tir à l'arc

تیراندازی با کمان

#726

fight

combattre

مبارزه کردن

#727

football

football

فوتبال

#728

cycling

cyclisme

دوچرخه‌سواری

#729

timer

minuteur

زمان‌سنج

#730

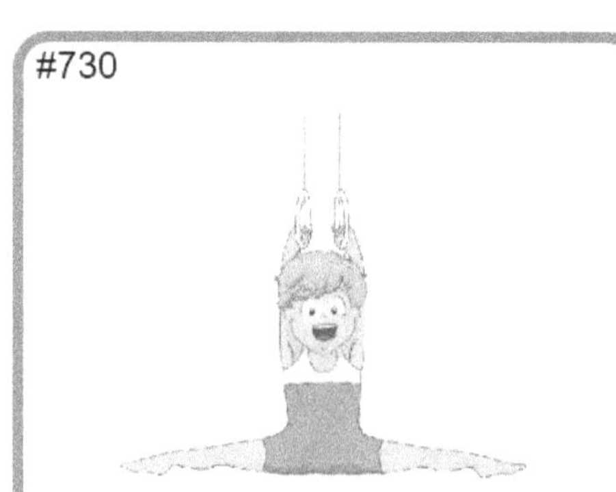

gymnastics

gymnastique

ژیمناستیک

#731

swimming

natation

شنا کردن

#732

wrestling

lutte

کشتی گرفتن

#733

jogging

jogging

دویدن آهسته

#734

climbing

escalade

کوهنوردی

#735

hopping

sautiller

پریدن

#736

surfing

surf

موج‌سواری

#737

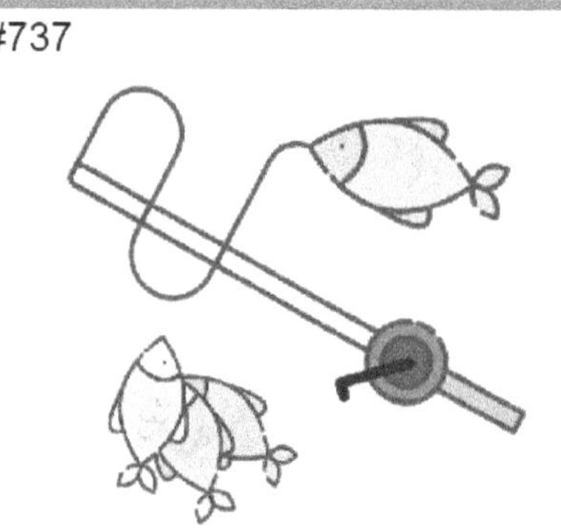

fishing

pêche

ماهیگیری

#738

racket

raquette

راکت

#739

dumbbells

haltères

دمبل

#740

ride

monter

سواری کردن

#741

soccer

football

فوتبال

#742

dance

danser

رقصیدن

#743

dive

plonger

غواصی کردن

#744

team

équipe

تیم

#745

boxing

boxe

بوکس

#746

kite

cerf-volant

بادبادک

#747

monday

lundi

دوشنبه

#748

thursday
jeudi
پنجشنبه

#749

wednesday
mercredi
چهارشنبه

#750

friday
vendredi
جمعه

#751

tuesday
mardi
سه‌شنبه

#752

saturday
samedi
شنبه

#753

sunday
dimanche
یکشنبه

#754

angel
ange
فرشته

#755

teacher
professeur
معلم

#756

leader
chef
رهبر

#757

politician

politicien

سیاستمدار

#758

king

roi

پادشاه

#759

judge

juge

قاضی

#760

actor

acteur

بازیگر

#761

chef

chef

سرآشپز

#762

nurse

infirmière

پرستار

#763

president

président

رئیس‌جمهور

#764

police

police

پلیس

#765

fisherman

pêcheur

ماهیگیر

#766

artist

artiste

هنرمند

#767

princess

princesse

شاهزاده خانم

#768

bartender

barman

ساقی

#769

waiter

serveur

پیشخدمت

#770

pharmacist

pharmacien

داروساز

#771

accountant

comptable

حسابدار

#772

barber

coiffeur

آرایشگر

#773

lawyer

avocat

وکیل

#774

policeman

policier

پلیس

#775

veterinarian

vétérinaire

دامپزشک

#776

cashier

caissier

صندوق‌دار

#777

entrepreneur

entrepreneur

کارآفرین

#778

singer

chanteur

خواننده

#779

ghost

fantôme

شبح

#780

bishop

évêque

اسقف

#781

knight

chevalier

شوالیه

#782

cop

flic

پلیس

#783

florist

fleuriste

گل‌فروش

#784

doctor

médecin

پزشک

#785

optician

opticien

عینک‌ساز

#786

driver

chauffeur

راننده

#787

queen

reine

ملکه

#788

witch

sorcière

جادوگر

#789

writer

écrivain

نویسنده

#790

army

armée

ارتش

#791

farmer

agriculteur

کشاورز

#792

boss

patron

رئیس

#793

plumber

plombier

لوله‌کش

#794

hairdresser

coiffeur

آرایشگر

#795

magician

magicien

جادوگر

#796

musician

musicien

موسیقیدان

#797

photographer

photographe

عکاس

#798

miner

mineur

معدنچی

#799

receptionist

réceptionniste

پذیرشگر

#800

pirate

pirate

دزد دریایی

#801

maid

bonne

خدمتکار

#802

carpenter

charpentier

نجار

#803

secretary

secrétaire

منشی

#804

baker

boulanger

نانوای

#805

butcher

boucher

قصاب

#806

pink

rose

صورتی

#807

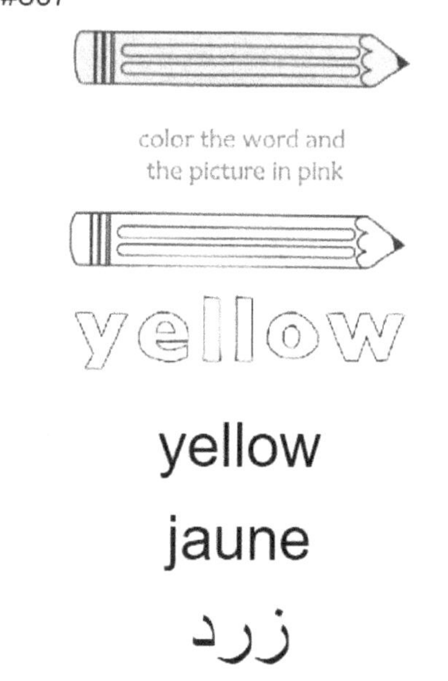

yellow

jaune

زرد

#808

brown

brun

قهوه‌ای

#809

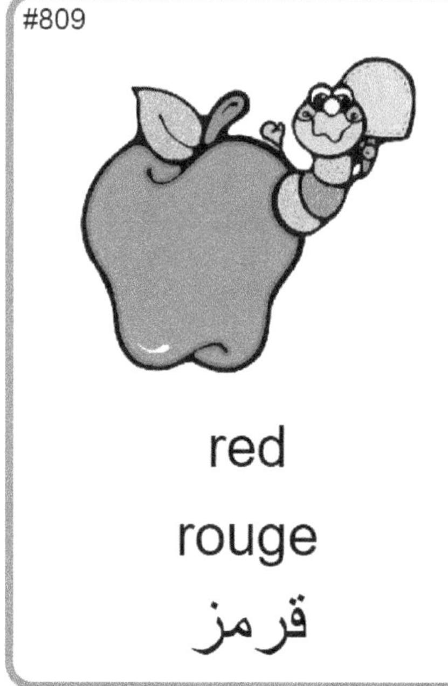

red

rouge

قرمز

#810

white

blanc

سفید

#811

gray

gris

خاکستری

#812

green

vert

سبز

#813

blue

bleu

آبی

#814

coast

côte

ساحل

#815

stormy

orageux

طوفانی

#816

moon

lune

ماه

#817

volcano

volcan

آتشفشان

#818

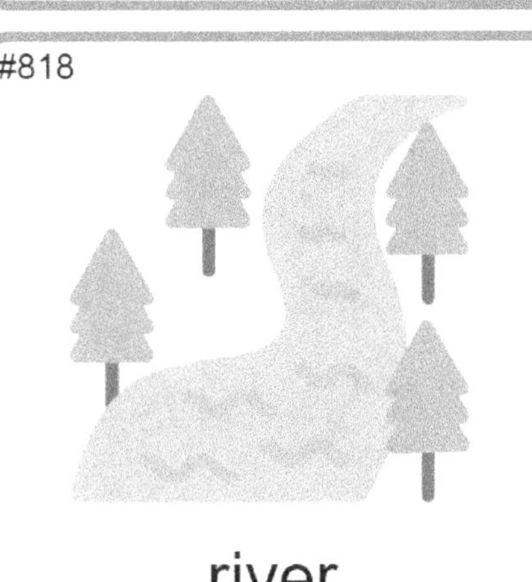

river

rivière

رودخانه

#819

foggy

brumeux

مه‌آلود

#820

rainy

pluvieux

بارانی

#821

heat

chaleur

حرارت

#822

cold

froid

سرد

#823

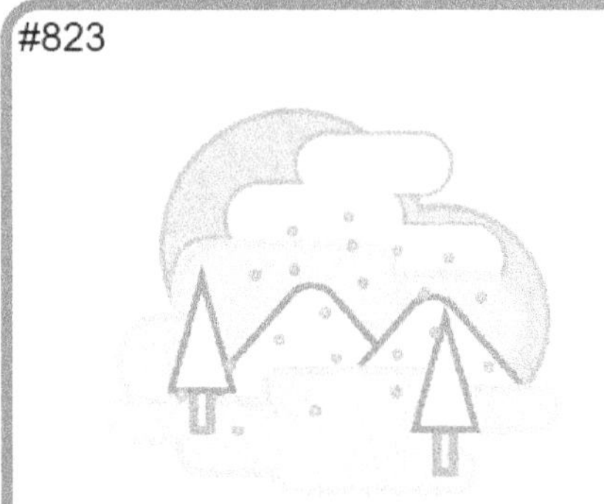

snowy

enneigé

برفی

#824

loud

fort

بلند

#825

windy

venteux

بادی

#826

wet

mouillé

خیس

#827

temperature

température

دما

#828

rainbow

arc-en-ciel

رنگین کمان

#829

steam

vapeur

بخار

#830
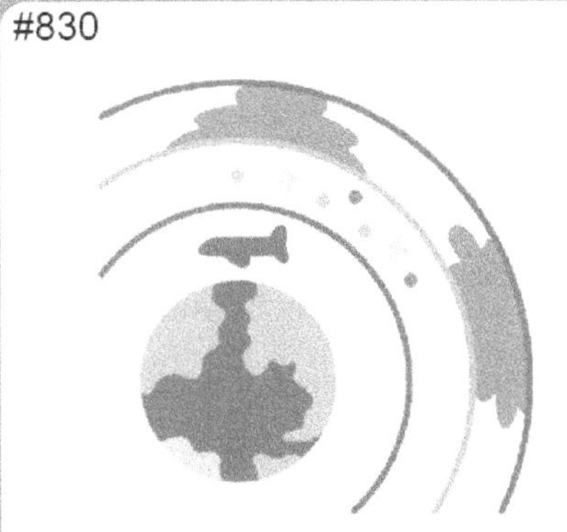

atmosphere

atmosphère

جو

#831

sea

mer

دریا

#832

mountain

montagne

کوه

#833

world

monde

جهان

#834

quiet

calme

ساکت

#835

disaster

désastre

فاجعه

#836

star

étoile

ستاره

#837

snow

neige

برف

#838

summer

été

تابستان

#839

sunny

ensoleillé

آفتابی

#840

cloudy

nuageux

ابری

#841

snowflake

flocon de neige

دانه برف

#842

dawn

aube

سپیده‌دم

#843

thunder

tonnerre

رعد و برق

#844

nature

nature

طبیعت

#845

sound

son

صدا

#846

rain

pluie

باران

#847

climate

climat

اقلیم

#848

lake

lac

دریاچه

#849

wave

vague

موج

#850

hot

chaud

داغ

#851

sun

soleil

خورشید

#852

location

emplacement

مکان

#853

smoke

fumée

دود

#854

humid

humide

مرطوب

#855

earth

terre

زمین

#856

year
année
سال

#857

night
nuit
شب

#858
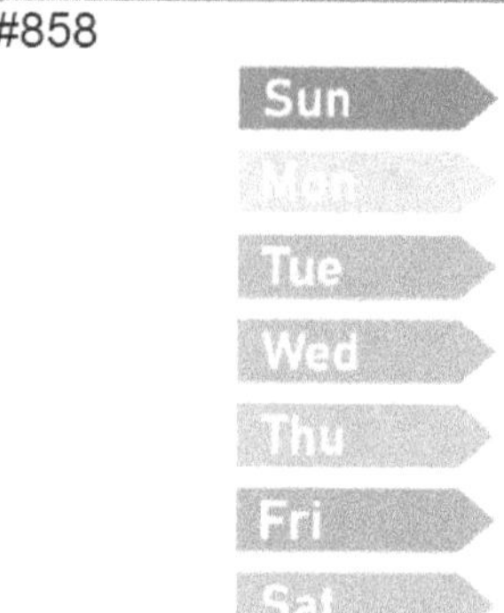
week
semaine
هفته

#859

morning
matin
صبح

#860

autumn
automne
پاییز

#861

midnight
minuit
نیمه‌شب

#862

time
temps
زمان

#863

month
mois
ماه

#864

noon
midi
ظهر

#865

day
jour
روز

#866

date
date
تاریخ

#867

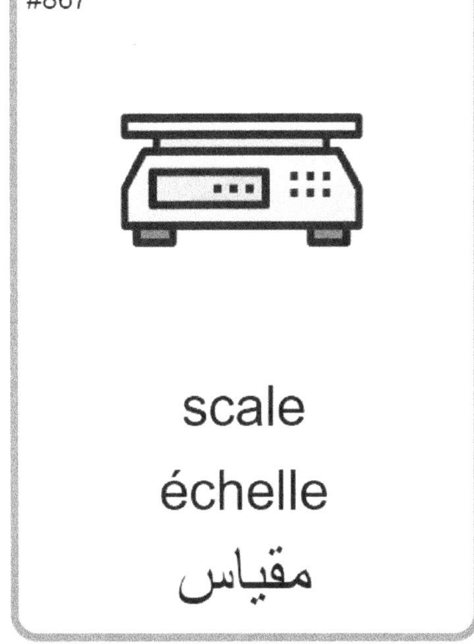

scale
échelle
مقیاس

#868

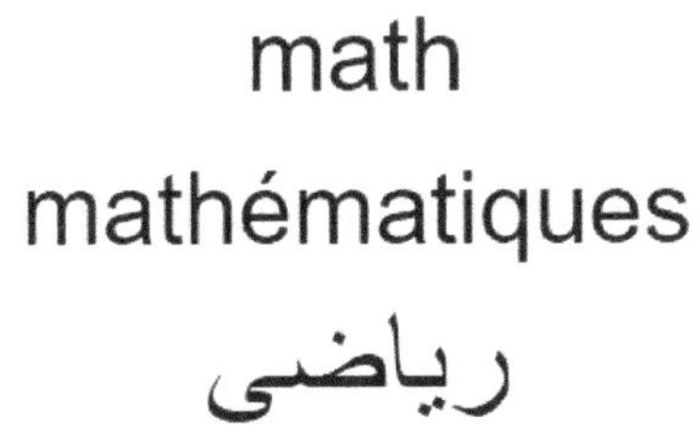

math
mathématiques
ریاضی

#869

painting
peinture
نقاشی

#870

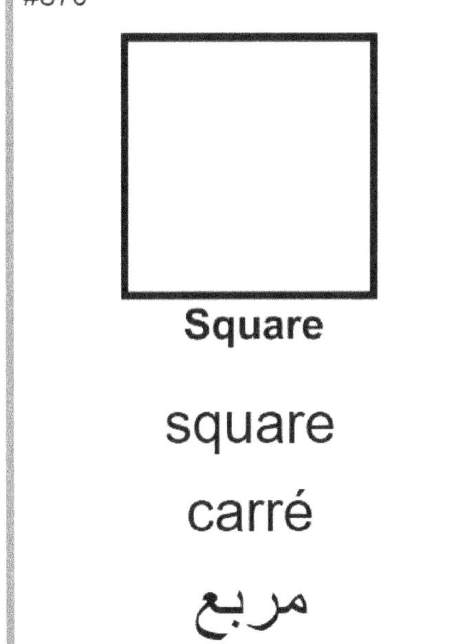

square
carré
مربع

#871

income
revenu
درآمد

#872

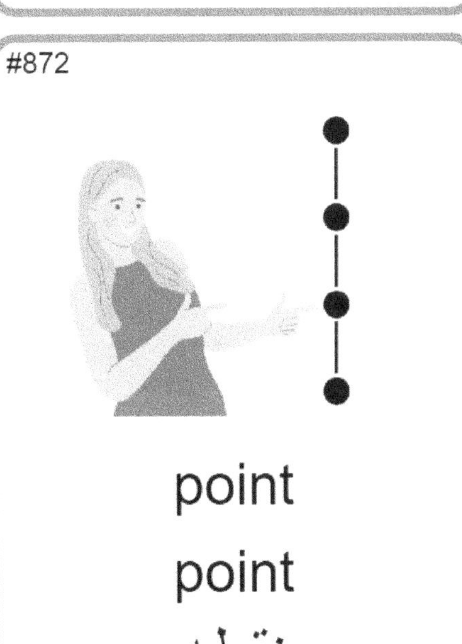

point
point
نقطه

#873

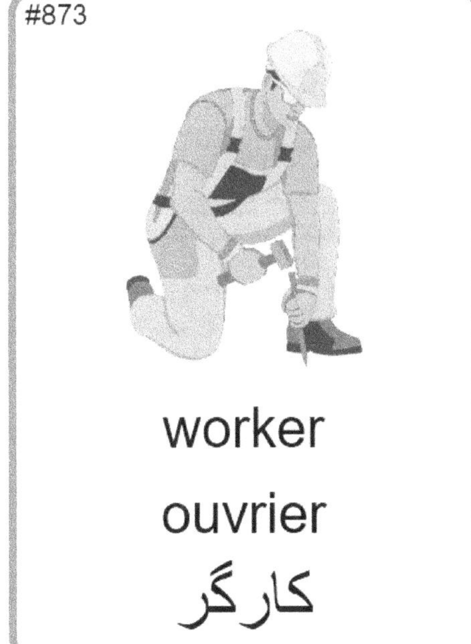

worker
ouvrier
کارگر

#874

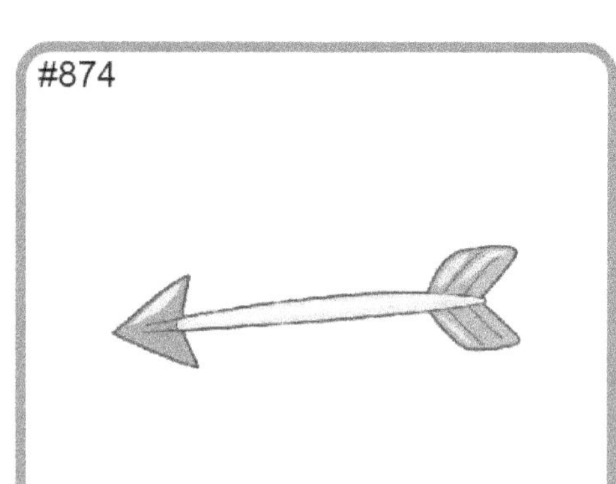

arrow

flèche

پیکان

#875

art

art

هنر

#876

country

pays

کشور

#877

customer

client

مشتری

#878

story

histoire

داستان

#879

homework

devoirs

تکلیف

#880

law

loi

قانون

#881

winner

gagnant

برنده

#882

passenger

passager

مسافر

#883

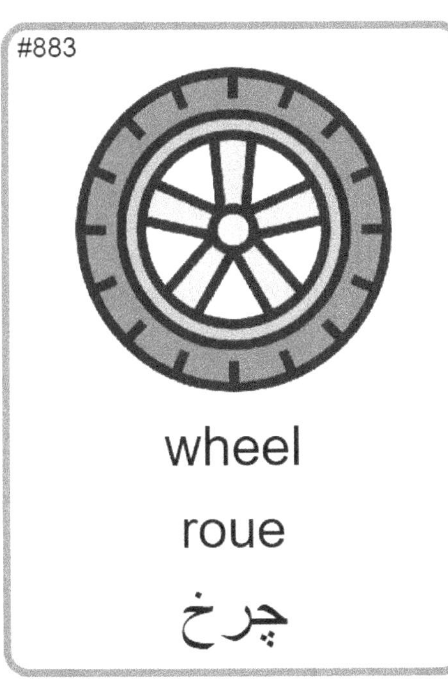

wheel

roue

چرخ

#884

news

nouvelles

اخبار

#885

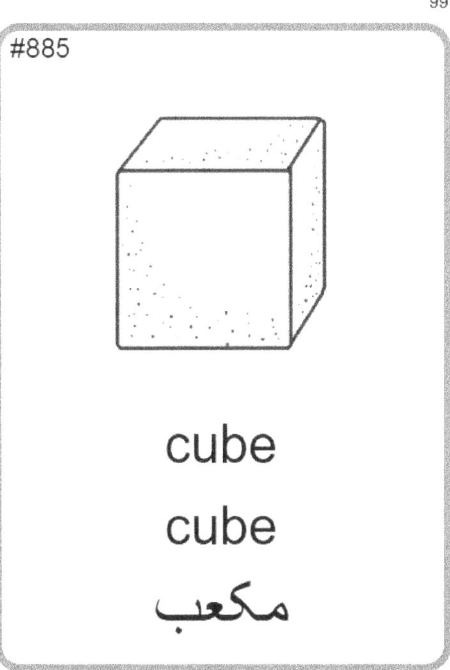

cube

cube

مکعب

#886

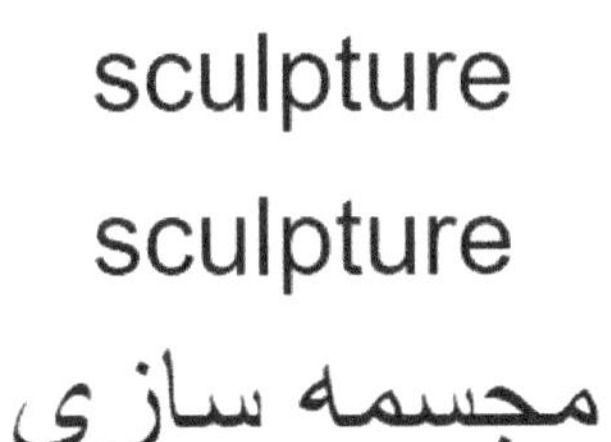

sculpture

sculpture

مجسمه سازی

#887

war

guerre

جنگ

#888

birthday

anniversaire

تولد

English French Persian

r k l i و ن g چ م u و o l t o
u i i x ا i n ی l e ی e u r p
i s g u گ d a e a p ر v e a ا
v s h n ی c ی m چ ی r r ش ن i
ه f t e c a o e p u e د د z s
p e b ج m u l w t o o a g ر ن n
i p u v ب b پ ش س ی u n e ی n
ت ب l e a ه r م r ه ش l r u r
b t b r u c د a ا t ف p e s x
o n ر e v o h د s ل د n ه l ن
i u r b f o q e q s ر چ س n ش
m ه n ر f p z م a e e r پ و i
د t é r ه c s u r ا و r ب و b
r ر e م v n ه e f n c r o d ه
u n x i m م i r h c n ی e م p

cow
vache
گاو

lightbulb
ampoule
لامپ

kiss
embrasser
بوسه

English French Persian

د i r x q i e ن c v c ه ی a u
چ x ه e e c ن g e ه e ج م r t
ر e ی b n m ه z l r ب x e ن r
t n ش a e g o r g e د م ن ه u
ا c a a م e ی ی ر و c ف c ه e
پ س e ب a h n a ن و ل ن l i a
a b ن r ی é t r r گ d د r e س
s k و a ر ن t w o a و e l ا ش
i e س a l l i g a t o r u t ا
o h د p e ا ا t ت v c r i x i
س ح ا س م ت e r a e و t و r a
c t b e ر ف x ی ک پ س ت ف o e
a o ب r ی i r ن ه z چ r r a e
o r a l l i g a t o r س n t r
w e é e d n d ن a x ا e e د م

throat

gorge

گلو

alligator

alligator

تمساح

two

deux

دو

English French Persian

e i a ر ی i z r e i c r p ف
q ن ت چ n r n b o ی t s a r
ه n o م s ا p n ر o c n e
i c پ r ج e ر پ ه ا t و ف م
ه i o g پ o م e و م i e r a c
i ا س n و z i o t ن u e ا ک
a ش c ر d u c k o م ه e b o e
ه ن c a n a r d d m گ a x n a
r س c و e t r ت d u q p ک ن n
f r e c p r r ر l r t ر د a و
ه o a گ ه o x r e پ o ا ر b x
r ک ص e o i r e r س و ش ا ا n
t o u t c p e t i t g ل g پ r
l t r o u s e r s ب e ش ه م a
ک t o e s م د e چ e ا r e د ش

toddler

tout-petit

پاپون

duck

canard

کدرا

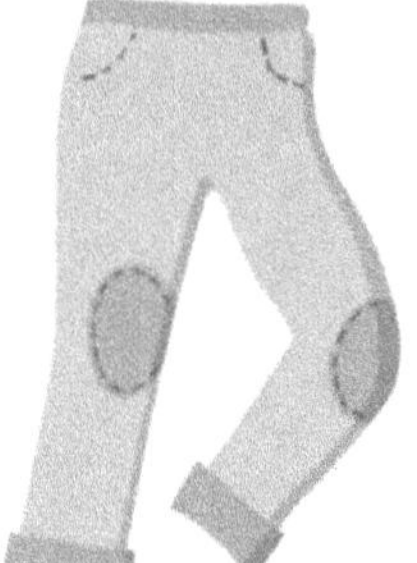

trousers

pantalon

شلوار

English French Persian

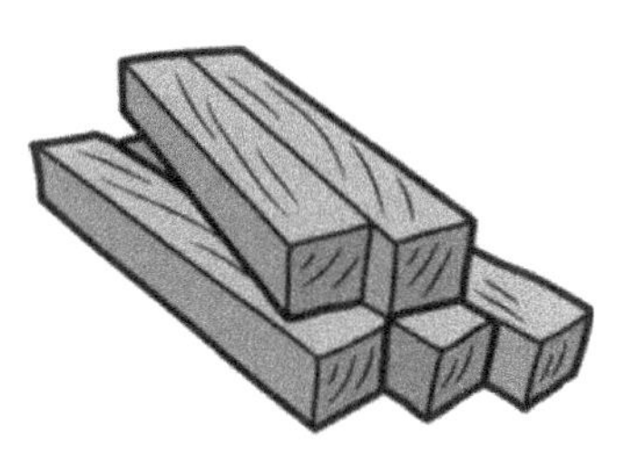
wood
bois
چوب

mug
tasse
ماگ

deer
cerf
گوزن

English French Persian

o ش e l e v e n v u ر س ر ر r ک
ه b e d i n o s a u r e و o t
r n p و f u c ا و a m c س v ی
ر e e r p ه د ز ا ی e s ا س t
s v t i ن ش u م ا e g e ن e ک
v ن e r ن ت e n x ا s u ی ص e
e r ا n ه ر t ا i i e s ا o م
x i e ح o b ه د i o t پ د ا r
a q i e ت n m e n ت و م r a ش
m e d v ن م z ن م v پ i i ش r
ف d e r p q ا e b s x u ب م r
ی n t i o e v r u e o س c v ن
s ت ر o b i e ش و e ش c b ن ف
d i n o s a u r و s n ا r e i
g e ا ت t e n c e a ی o t و ف

exam
examen
امتحان

eleven
onze
یازده

dinosaur
dinosaure
دایناسور

English French Persian

و e z e a p p r é c i e r م o
ر s ا پ ش ی v r r o ش p o ا a x
ه v e د r ی چ f c s ب n ا f
p e o ن r چ i r t u ی v f i ب
x u i د ی t r k r b r ن t t ع
o e t ر l p l a t e a u ی p ک
m س r ب i r چ ک c ا ه s e م
p n i ت f ف k s u ی l u i ن u
a e د ذ s ن r l b d ک e ت ه v
e م n ل i n ر س e b r م o س
r ن o j l e z ا t r a y ی t ا
ن e i r o p u r c پ i x o o l
x o ر ا l y i n s u n a ب ن e
e u e س e م e ا د ک t a c ج n
م d ن ت i t p f e ب ف e i گ م

tray

plateau

سینی

enjoy

apprécier

لذت بردن

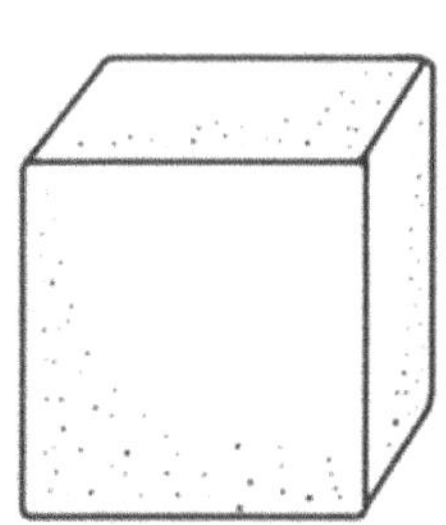

cube

cube

مکعب

English French Persian

q x e a ت s x c د r ی b a e t
f u v l g x ر i n o ق ر l q ن
r s a e س p c ا s م g ه i e f
g p و r n چ v p ه ن l t p r l
f ر ی o a t e و د چ ن x t g o
r o f l ش n i r e w و a ا a r
ا p r c i و t l t k ه ل e c i
r و n t r a ر e a و ت ک ه د s
ر o o e y س ن ف f t د i ن چ t
t n i t c f r i q e ه v پ o
ف ا t ت n o ن e ل u u n n i
o e c e م w c u f t گ a r i a
t e d c e c م م r a i o t n و
t f l e u r i s t e n e e r u
e پ ت t r t د ش o ک o ن ه i u e

fan
ventilateur
پنکه

florist
fleuriste
گل‌فروش

forty four
quarante-quatre
چهل و چهار

د e v s n f g é n e r g i e i
l o n پ n ا a e و ک x ن p a
c ر i e پ g k ى s r r n a p u
n ه s م r v o p e پ p e a پ t
x i i u b g ک ه i e d k س c پ
ر s x c پ l y ت ى ه ه i a د a
ش p t x t ر a ش و s ق i r ى س
c ش y w ت ا i n b e s e چ ف b
l ا e h o ن e و c e ت پ k س n
پ د i i ا ه r ت t چ z k c p i
c r g t a b ى ص ر l G e د v
ن u h e c p چ ش r é t r پ e s
ش t t e ن ا r ى م a i r r ج r
ا s o i x a n t e ر h u i t e
ا l پ r e v é t ى ژ ن ر n م

sixty eight

soixante-huit

شصت و هشت

white

blanc

سفید

energy

énergie

انرژی

English French Persian

e ن ر u ف ی و د t ه u i r ن e
r s o ف x e a ه ا e m e a v a
ت a ت p o e p ن v i ا u z پ a
c r s p r o م r ا e ف f o g f
ت ا ی o ی a ر e u r n a r ن i
ف r ت و i ر c د e c e ن e v f
ه ا پ ی n r t t i t a i z c t
و ه ه r ل د c n i r c ن t ن y
ه ت ا n v ا ن t ه v t r ر s s
ا f n c t د ع ا c ه i d e o e
ج r س ی e ا a ف s o v t i و v
ن ب e م ر س غ r o م i c é ص e
پ u o c é r ن ی i م t u c p n
و c ی r c p b ش ت a y x z س و
c i n q u a n t e i s e p t o

activity

activité

فعالیت

razor

rasoir

تیغ

fifty seven

cinquante-sept

پنجاه و هفت

English French Persian

c ت a د o i l پ م e l e n ا d m
س e e u ا f د و ر ه o e t n ا
o s r r ا L o g i ا o c h ی و
o n e v ه e ا u i م ه ه e e e
ت د v w e p x س r ش t چ v o t
g e u n د a ر a c q t ا ر ن ن
u ش ل l r o u u ک و u t x h a ا
ر ا b r a i n n n a e e r f ز
م ب e م q i ا b e t o o i s غ
t s a o ا s ل e q r a i n a م
q ر a a f e ت e ه e ک م c l g
a q o l r c ن n e ش i r r a v
ه م s t a e r r i n h i p d e
ف ت e t م d و ی ش ی و v ن e i
م ا و ر د پ ر t ک ن e l p i t

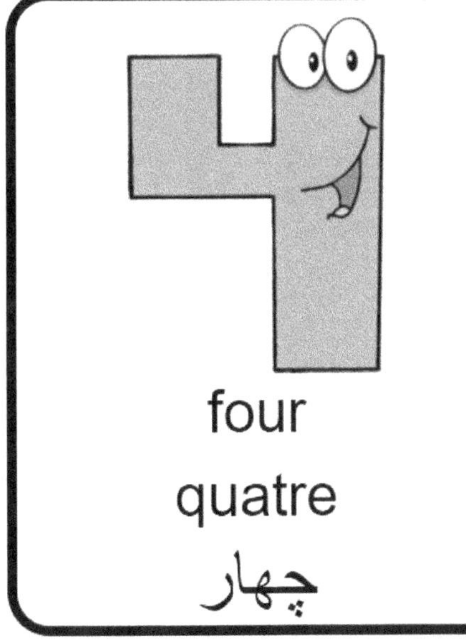

four

quatre

چهار

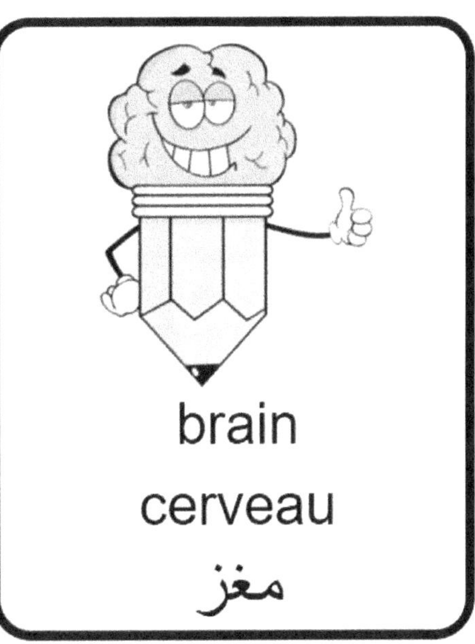

brain

cerveau

مغز

salad

salade

سالاد